RON KOVIC

GREAT ACHIEVERS

LIVES OF THE PHYSICALLY CHALLENGED

RON KOVIC

ANTIWAR ACTIVIST

Nathaniel Moss

Chelsea House Publishers

New York • Philadelphia

CHELSEA HOUSE PUBLISHERS

EDITORIAL DIRECTOR   Richard Rennert
EXECUTIVE MANAGING EDITOR   Karyn Gullen Browne
EXECUTIVE EDITOR   Sean Dolan
COPY CHIEF   Robin James
PICTURE EDITOR   Adrian G. Allen
ART DIRECTOR   Robert Mitchell
MANUFACTURING DIRECTOR   Gerald Levine
PRODUCTION COORDINATOR   Marie Claire Cebrián-Ume

GREAT ACHIEVERS: LIVES OF THE PHYSICALLY CHALLENGED

SENIOR EDITOR   Kathy Kuhtz

Staff for **RON KOVIC**

ASSOCIATE EDITOR   Martin Schwabacher
EDITORIAL ASSISTANTS   Kelsey Goss and Mary B. Sisson
PICTURE RESEARCHER   Alan Gottlieb
SERIES DESIGN   Basia Niemczyc
COVER ILLUSTRATION   Alex Zwarenstein

First Printing

1   3   5   7   9   8   6   4   2

Library of Congress Cataloging-in-Publication Data

Moss, Nathaniel
Ron Kovic / Nathaniel Moss
p. cm.—(Great achievers)
Includes bibliographical references and index.
Summary: A biography of the young veteran who wrote of his struggle to create a
meaningful life after being crippled during the Vietnam War.
ISBN 0-7910-2076-2
    0-7910-2089-4 (pbk.)
1. Kovic, Ron—Juvenile literature. 2. Paraplegics—United States—Biography—
Juvenile literature.   3. Vietnamese Conflict, 1961–1975—Personal narratives,
American—Juvenile literature. 4. Vietnamese Conflict, 1961–1975—Veterans—
United States—Biography—Juvenile literature. [1. Kovic, Ron. 2. Paraplegics. 3.
Physically handicapped. 4. Veterans. 5. Vietnamese Conflict, 1961–1975—Veter-
ans.] I. Title. II. Series: Great achievers (Chelsea House Publishers)
RC406.P3K685 1993   93-16373
362.1'9758'0092—dc20   CIP
[B]   AC

CONTENTS

GREAT ACHIEVERS

LIVES OF THE PHYSICALLY CHALLENGED

A MESSAGE FOR EVERYONE

Jerry Lewis

Just 44 years ago—when I was the ripe old age of 23—an incredible stroke of fate rocketed me to overnight stardom as an entertainer. After the initial shock wore off, I began to have a very strong feeling that, in return for all life had given me, I must find a way of giving something back. At just that moment, a deeply moving experience in my personal life persuaded me to take up the leadership of a fledgling battle to defeat a then little-known group of diseases called muscular dystrophy, as well as other related neuromuscular diseases—all of which are disabling and, in the worst cases, cut life short.

In 1950, when the Muscular Dystrophy Association (MDA)—of which I am national chairman—was established, physical disability was looked on as a matter of shame. Franklin Roosevelt, who guided America through World War II from a wheelchair, and Harold Russell, the World War II hero who lost both hands in battle, then became an Academy Award–winning movie star and chairman of the President's Committee on Employment of the Handicapped, were the exceptions. One of the reasons that muscular dystrophy and related diseases were so little known was that people who had been disabled by them were hidden at home, away from the pity and discomfort with which they were generally regarded by society. As I got to know and began working with people who have disabilities, I quickly learned what a tragic mistake this perception was. And my determination to correct this terrible problem

7

soon became as great as my commitment to see disabling neuromuscular diseases wiped from the face of the earth.

I have long wondered why it never occurs to us, as we experience the knee-jerk inclination to feel sorry for people who are physically disabled, that lives such as those led by President Roosevelt, Harold Russell, and all of the extraordinary people profiled in this Great Achievers series demonstrate unmistakably how wrong we are. Physical disability need not be something that blights life and destroys opportunity for personal fulfillment and accomplishment. On the contrary, as people such as Ray Charles, Stephen Hawking, and Ron Kovic prove, physical disability can be a spur to greatness rather than a condemnation of emptiness.

In fact, if my experience with physically disabled people can be taken as a guide, as far as accomplishment is concerned, they have a slight edge on the rest of us. The unusual challenges they face require finding greater-than-average sources of energy and determination to achieve much of what able-bodied people take for granted. Often, this ultimately translates into a lifetime of superior performance in whatever endeavor people with disabilities choose to pursue.

If you have watched my Labor Day Telethon over the years, you know exactly what I am talking about. Annually, we introduce to tens of millions of Americans people whose accomplishments would distinguish them regardless of their physical conditions—top-ranking executives, physicians, scientists, lawyers, musicians, and artists. The message I hope the audience receives is not that these extraordinary individuals have achieved what they have by overcoming a dreadful disadvantage that the rest of us are lucky not to have to endure. Rather, I hope our viewers reflect on the fact that these outstanding people have been ennobled and strengthened by the tremendous challenges they have faced.

In 1992, MDA, which has grown over the past four decades into one of the world's leading voluntary health agencies, established a personal achievement awards program to demonstrate to the nation that the distinctive qualities of people with disabilities are by no means confined to the famous. What could have been more appropriate or timely in that year of the implementation of the 1990 Americans with Disabilities Act than to take an action that could perhaps finally achieve the alteration of public perception of disability, which MDA had struggled over four decades to achieve?

On Labor Day, 1992, it was my privilege to introduce to America MDA's inaugural national personal achievement award winner, Steve Mikita, assistant attorney general of the state of Utah. Steve graduated magna cum laude from Duke University as its first wheelchair student in history and was subsequently named the outstanding young lawyer of the year by the Utah Bar Association. After he spoke on the Telethon with an eloquence that caused phones to light up from coast to coast, people asked me where he had been all this time and why they had not known of him before, so deeply impressed were they by him. I answered that he and thousands like him have been here all along. We just have not adequately *noticed* them.

It is my fervent hope that we can eliminate indifference once and for all and make it possible for all of our fellow citizens with disabilities to gain their rightfully high place in our society.

ON FACING CHALLENGES

John Callahan

I was paralyzed for life in 1972, at the age of 21. A friend and I were driving in a Volkswagen on a hot July night, when he smashed the car at full speed into a utility pole. He suffered only minor injuries. But my spinal cord was severed during the crash, leaving me without any feeling from my diaphragm downward. The only muscles I could move were some in my upper body and arms, and I could also extend my fingers. After spending a lot of time in physical therapy, it became possible for me to grasp a pen.

I've always loved to draw. When I was a kid, I made pictures of everything from Daffy Duck (one of my lifelong role models) to caricatures of my teachers and friends. I've always been a people watcher, it seems; and I've always looked at the world in a sort of skewed way. Everything I see just happens to translate immediately into humor. And so, humor has become my way of coping. As the years have gone by, I have developed a tremendous drive to express my humor by drawing cartoons.

The key to cartooning is to put a different spin on the expected, the normal. And that's one reason why many of my cartoons deal with the disabled: amputees, quadriplegics, paraplegics, the blind. The public is not used to seeing them in cartoons.

But there's another reason why my subjects are often disabled men and women. I'm sick and tired of people who presume to speak for the disabled. Call me a cripple, call me a gimp, call me paralyzed for life.

Just don't call me something I'm not. I'm not "differently abled," and my cartoons show that disabled people should not be treated any differently than anyone else.

All of the men, women, and children who are profiled in the Great Achievers series share this in common: their various handicaps have not prevented them from accomplishing great things. Their life stories are worth knowing about because they have found the strength and courage to develop their talents and to follow their dreams as fully as they can.

Whether able-bodied or disabled, a person must strive to overcome obstacles. There's nothing greater than to see a person who faces challenges and conquers them, regardless of his or her limitations.

In a triumphant moment, Ron Kovic receives applause from the delegates at the 1976 Democratic National Convention in New York and a hug from Fritz Efaw, an advocate of amnesty for draft dodgers whose nomination for vice-president Kovic seconded in a nationally televised speech.

1

AMERICA'S YANKEE DOODLE DANDY

WHEN RON KOVIC GENTLY PUSHED his wheelchair into the spotlight of New York's Madison Square Garden on the evening of July 15, 1976, he had reached the end of a long journey. Raised to believe in God and his country, Ron had eagerly enlisted in the marines after his senior year in high school and had gone off to fight a vague menace, the Vietcong, halfway around the world in Vietnam. Like many of the boys of his generation, he had grown up with the films of John Wayne and Audie Murphy, whose daring and bravery in such films as *The Sands of Iwo Jima* and *To Hell and Back* had made war look glamorous.

For Ron Kovic, this patriotic calling might have seemed inevitable. After all, how many people could say they were born on the Fourth of July? He had grown up celebrating his birthday on the same day that his country commemorated its own birth, and that made him proud.

Kovic's father had fought for his country in World War II against Nazi Germany and its allies, and young Ron, who was born in 1946, just a year after the victory over Hitler's Germany, considered it his generation's duty to do the same when its turn was called.

But nothing could have prepared Kovic for what awaited him in Vietnam. Throughout his first tour of duty, Ron maintained the cocksure optimism that marine training had instilled in him and his fellow recruits—an optimism generated in part from earnest patriotism and naïveté about war and reinforced by a fortuitous avoidance of heavy artillery fire. On his second tour, Ron's luck would run out. After suffering a wound to his left foot, Kovic took on a group of enemy soldiers in a fierce display of bravado. For his heroic efforts he was rewarded with a single bullet through his shoulder. The slug shattered Kovic's spine, leaving him helpless on the battlefield, paralyzed from the chest down.

It was now nearly a decade later and Kovic, just turned 30, had a message for the American people. He simply needed the appropriate forum in which to deliver it, and the 1976 Democratic National Convention provided precisely that.

The Democratic delegates were buoyant this year, convinced that the presidency was within their grasp again for the first time since Hubert Humphrey had suffered defeat at the hands of Richard Nixon in 1968. Nixon had won again in 1972. But much had changed since then, most notably the revelation of President Nixon's participation in illegal campaign activities during the 1972 election. Those actions, which included illegal wiretapping of Democratic opponents, the solicitation of unlawful campaign contributions, use of the Central Intelligence Agency (CIA) for domestic spying purposes, and the now-famous attempted burglary of campaign materials from Senator George McGovern's election headquarters, came to be known collectively as Watergate, after the Washington,

On April 29, 1974, President Richard M. Nixon sits before a stack of transcripts of taped conversations containing evidence about the Watergate scandal. Nixon was driven from office after his attempts to cover up the "dirty tricks" committed by his reelection committee were exposed.

D.C., hotel and office complex in which McGovern rented space for his campaign.

Rather than face almost certain impeachment proceedings, a humiliation suffered only once before in the nation's history when Congress attempted unsuccessfully to remove Andrew Johnson from office in 1868, President Nixon had resigned. Though Nixon had escaped impeachment, his resignation left a scar on the psyche of the American public. The leaders of the Democratic party, well aware of the country's distaste for Nixon's abuses of power, used the scandal to their advantage during their campaign. The Democratic convention was a big part of that strategy.

The controversy that had surrounded Democratic conventions of previous election years had been carefully avoided: the chaos of 1964, when the party elders refused to seat Fanny Lou Hamer and the other black delegates from the Mississippi Freedom Democratic party who challenged the lopsided racial makeup of their state's representatives in Atlantic City; the riots in Chicago in 1968, when Mayor Richard Daley unleashed the Illinois National Guard on thousands of young men and women protesting the party's support for the Vietnam War; and

The brutality of the police's response to demonstrations by youthful antiwar protesters during the 1968 Democratic National Convention in Chicago put a cloud over the nomination of Hubert Humphrey, the Democratic candidate for president.

the triumphant liberalism displayed before the nation in Miami just four years earlier, when McGovern accepted the party's nomination only to face a landslide defeat at the hands of President Nixon in November.

This convention was elaborately choreographed. The party leaders were convinced that if the Democrats could simply present themselves as a respectable alternative to the Republicans, who had brought disgrace to the presidency and embarrassment to the American people, they would have no problems in November.

But the millions of people watching the convention on their television sets at home had something else on their minds as well. After years of seeing the nation torn apart over the Vietnam War, Americans were eager to begin the process of healing. The last U.S. troops had left Vietnam

in 1973, and Saigon had fallen two years later. As Jerry
Parker wrote for *New York Newsday,* "for most Americans,
the Vietnam nightmare was over." Democratic success
depended at least in part on the ability to convince the
American people that in Georgia governor Jimmy Carter
they had a man who could move them forward into a new
era of peace and honest government.

The convention, although uneventful, had run smoothly
through the first three nights. The excitement over whom
Carter would nominate as his vice-presidential candidate
had been resolved only that morning, with the selection of
Senator Walter Mondale of Minnesota. All that was left to
do was to make Senator Mondale's nomination formal
from the podium of the convention that evening. Afterward, Carter would speak, and the convention would
adjourn.

But there were others whose names would be placed in
nomination for vice-president that Thursday evening. One
was Fritz Efaw, a draft resister who had spent the duration
of the Vietnam War in England and who had only recently
returned. Though they had no chance of success, the names
of Efaw and two others, Representative Ron Dellums and
Gary Benoit, were to be placed in nomination in a symbolic
gesture to give voice to their respective concerns.

Efaw's message related to the issue of amnesty for the
men who had dodged the draft for the Vietnam War, as
well as the men who had received dishonorable discharges
for deserting the army when their consciences no longer
allowed them to participate. The majority of Democratic
delegates gathered in Madison Square Garden supported
the amnesty, as did Carter (who would later grant an
unconditional pardon after becoming president). But before Efaw could make his case, his name had to be placed
in nomination and then seconded by another speaker. Who
could be better qualified to speak out in support of men
who had evaded the draft than Ron Kovic, a man who had
served his country in Vietnam and had seen with his own

eyes what was happening there, a man for whom the Vietnam nightmare was most definitely not over?

As Kovic moved into place on the speaker's platform, he understood the importance of what he was about to do no less than he understood the struggle he had undertaken during the past nine years. Kovic knew as well as anyone that the battle fought on the beaches and in the jungles of Vietnam was being fought all over again by thousands of returning veterans: for acceptance, for respect, for understanding, and for healing.

Kovic had experienced the horror of the conditions in the veterans' hospitals, where men crippled by the war suffered daily indignities while ever more money was being spent on the war. He had witnessed the suffering of other men like him, who because of their paralysis could never express their sexuality the way other men could. He understood the depression and anger that came with their

On July 15, 1976, Ron Kovic began his speech before the Democratic National Convention in New York City with a poem that read:

> *I am the living death*
> *the memorial day on wheels*
> *I am your yankee doodle dandy*
> *your john wayne come home*
> *your fourth of july firecracker*
> *exploding in the grave.*

physical and emotional injury. In short, he knew what the war had taken from him and countless others and that finding a way out of serving was no more a sign of cowardice than fighting the war had been a sign of bravery.

Four years earlier, Kovic and hundreds of other members of the Vietnam Veterans Against the War (VVAW) had gathered in Miami, Florida, at the Republican convention of 1972. He and two others had entered the convention uninvited and had tried to shout down the president. Now Kovic sat before thousands of delegates at another convention as an honored guest. He did not have to shout to be heard. A microphone would carry his voice to the giant audience packed inside the arena and the millions of viewers watching at home on their television sets.

As Lee Ewing described the scene for the *National Observer:* "The delegates had been in a jocular mood, laughing, talking, tossing a ball overhead, ignoring the calls for order. But when Kovic spoke the milling thousands in Madison Square Garden grew still and listened."

Ron opened with a poem that captured the hearts and minds of all who listened, and with which he had opened his celebrated autobiography, *Born on the Fourth of July.* "I am the living death," he began slowly, "the memorial day on wheels/I am your yankee doodle dandy/your john wayne come home/your fourth of july firecracker/exploding in the grave."

Kovic described his pain when he first heard of draft resisters burning their cards. He described his further pain when "I shot and killed a man. When he was pulled in, I suddenly realized I had accidentally killed one of my own men." That experience and his treatment upon returning home, said Kovic, had turned him around. His views had changed from blind patriotism to angry opposition toward a war that had left him "with legs that would not stand, a body that would not feel and a pain that never seemed to leave me." He went on to issue a strong plea for amnesty. After Kovic and Efaw embraced upon the stage, they

Ron Kovic (center, holding flag) and two other disabled veterans lead a demonstration by the Vietnam Veterans Against the War (VVAW) outside the Republican National Convention in Miami on August 21, 1972.

received tremendous, loud applause. *Time* magazine described the scene as one of the few poignant moments during the convention, and many in the audience were brought to tears.

Kovic appreciated the opportunity to help the people of his country to see what had happened, and what was still happening, to America's veterans. As he put it bluntly in a later interview, "It was the biggest moment in my life, the vindication of all the years that the government had tried to shut me up, to spit in my face. I was addressing the whole U.S.A."

If Kovic sounded bitter, it was hard to argue that it was not justified. He had been struggling to give meaning to his injury ever since he had returned home from the war, his body twisted and half-dead, in the spring of 1968. He had seen John Wayne's portrayal of a heroic soldier in the film *The Green Berets* when it was released later that year. Kovic feared that other high school students would be taken in by Wayne's romanticized exploits on screen, just as he had been. "When I left the theater," Kovic said later in a 1990 interview, "I told a friend that was not the way it was. I had been there."

Coming to terms with the difference between Hollywood's vision of war and the reality he experienced was perhaps the most difficult adjustment for Kovic. "I felt cheated, lied to, misled, deceived!" Kovic recalled. "I was enraged, I was furious, I was frustrated, I was frightened, I felt devastated. I demanded justice. I felt completely devoid of connection with others around me. And I felt a desperate need to assert myself. I was drowning in a sea of lies and a whirlpool of injustice."

On July 4, 1976, the United States turned 200 years old, and Ron Kovic turned 30. By the time he addressed his fellow delegates at the Democratic National Convention two weeks later, he had gone a long way toward correcting the false impressions many Americans still had about the war and asserting himself as he had longed to do. He had not become the John Wayne–type hero he had dreamed of being as a boy. Instead he had become a very different kind of hero. Like Thomas Jefferson, who shared his birthday, Ron Kovic had become a true patriot, a patriot of conscience holding the nation to the constitutional principles upon which it was founded.

It was a triumphant moment, one that would perhaps be equaled in his lifetime but never surpassed. The Democrats went on to victory that year with the election of Jimmy Carter to the presidency. It was the dawn of a new era, the "post-Vietnam" era, and Ron Kovic had helped to usher it in.

Ron Kovic was in many ways the archetypal all-American boy. A fine athlete, he competed for his high school's wrestling, track, and soccer teams.

2

LIFE IN
MASSAPEQUA

RON KOVIC WAS BORN in Ladysmith, Wisconsin, on July 4, 1946. If Kovic would enter Madison Square Garden 30 years later as part of a clearly identifiable grouping—the Vietnam Generation—he nevertheless entered the world as a member of another equally well-defined generation. He was a baby boomer. World War II had ended, and an era in American life marked by economic and social prosperity had begun. Historians would later acknowledge that the so-called abundance of the postwar years had been overstated. Many middle-class families, however, achieved a new standard of living in America's growing suburban communities.

It was in 1952 that the Kovic family moved into one of these communities—in Massapequa, Long Island, in New York. Ron's father, a checker at a local supermarket, worked 12-hour days, 6 days a week, to give his family the opportunity to achieve the middle-class status that now seemed the birthright of every American. Unlike his

Actor John Wayne symbolized the American ideal of masculinity for a generation, starring in numerous movies that presented military service and warfare as heroic.

parents' depression-era generation, Ron's youth was relatively unencumbered by economic worries. The Kovic children were well provided for. Ron's parents, Eli and Patricia Kovic, had six children. Suzanne was the oldest, then came Ronnie, Tommy, Patty, Jimmy, and Jack. Ron fondly recalls sitting around the breeakfast table reading the comics as his father whipped up a delicious breakfast of eggs and hash browns, "filling our bellies and making us feel warm and good inside."

As a young boy his greatest anxiety was whether the Yankees would win the pennant. Kovic's best friend, Richie Castiglia, would come over to watch Yankee games on the Kovics' television set—the Castiglias had yet to purchase their own—and they waited in eager anticipation for their favorite Bronx Bomber, Mickey Mantle, to step to the plate. Kovic recalls that "when Mantle hit a homer you could hear the TV halfway down the block. Richie and I would go completely nuts hugging each other and jumping up and down with tears streaming down our faces."

Kovic himself loved to play ball—both in stickball games along Hamilton Avenue on summer evenings and in the local Massapequa Little League. On his first time up at bat in Little League, Kovic hit a home run, racing around the bases—like his major league heroes—as his teammates yelled with excitement. Playing catch-a-fly-you're-up with another buddy, Kenny Goodman, young Ronny took over for Yankee announcer Mel Allen, screaming to an imaginary radio audience, "Did you see that, folks?! Kovic has just made a tremendous catch and the crowd is going wild." In Kovic's mind, "I was Mickey Mantle, Willie Mays, and all my other heroes, rolled into one."

If Mantle and Mays had achieved the status of the gods, they were not alone. Television had brought the exploits of a wide range of human endeavor right into the homes of average Americans. Hollywood, the space race, and the growth of pop music gave a young boy of the 1950s a wide range of heroes to select from. But no one captivated

Kovic's imagination more than film star John Wayne, whose brave exploits came to symbolize selfless heroism in Ron's mind.

Ron saw *The Sands of Iwo Jima* with his friend Richie, and the two of them sat rapt in the theater as Sergeant Stryker, played by Wayne, martyred himself for the cause of victory in the South Pacific. With tears in their eyes, Richie and Ron hummed along with the Marine Corps hymn as they watched the U.S. soldiers raising the flag over Iwo Jima—a heroic battle to be sure, but one of the bloodiest too, costing thousands of American lives. When Kovic saw the Audie Murphy picture *To Hell and Back*, he was similarly moved. "At the end," he remembers,

> he jumps on top of a flaming tank that's just about to explode and grabs the machine gun blasting it into the German lines. He was so brave I had chills running up and down my back, wishing it were me up there.

Ron and his friends spent countless hours in the woods near their neighborhood replaying the scenes from the adventurous war movies they watched at Sunday matinees. With battery-operated machine guns and other high-tech toy artillery of the time, the boys set up ambushes, led heroic attacks, and went off on reconnaissance patrols behind German lines, "bayonetting and shooting anyone who got in our way."

With Richie Castiglia and Bobby Zimmer, Ron would seize the cannon across from the American Legion hall down by Sparky's barbershop. They would sit on the cannon with their guns and canteens, waiting for a train to pull into the Massapequa railway station just across the way. Then, with all the fury and courage they could muster, the three boys would cry, "Ambush!" before riddling the train's windows with imaginary fire from the cannon and their machine guns. Ron and Richie also launched mock raids on a local housing project with plastic grenades and Matty Mattel rapid-fire guns. They studied the Marine

Bobby Zimmer, Ron Kovic's childhood friend, shared Ron's delight in playing war games with the other local boys. One of their favorite sites for mock battles was Massapequa's American Legion hall, which kept a cannon on its front lawn.

Corps guidebook and dreamed of going to the Levittown recruiting station to sign up when they turned 17.

Indeed, Kovic was eager to grow up and become a man, perhaps a bit too eager. He has described himself as impatient in school—the kind of boy who looked dreamily out the window, anxious for the year to end and the summer to begin. If Kovic had more important things on his mind than doing his homework, certainly one of those things was his devotion to God and his Catholic religious training. Ron prayed every evening before bed to God, to Jesus, and to the Virgin Mary that he would grow up to be a good American. The intensity of his devotion was so great that he sometimes even made himself cry. With God, thought Kovic, the world was full of possibility. Perhaps God would help Ron achieve his great dreams. "I made my first Holy Communion," he later wrote, "with a cowboy hat on my head and two six-shooters in my hands."

As Kovic grew older and entered high school he became preoccupied, as is typical in adolescence, with his body and with physical challenges. Besides playing baseball and war games, Ron prided himself on his agility. He could finesse a flip off the backyard fence as easily as he could walk on his hands. He loved to swim and ride his bike. In contrast to his boredom in the classroom, Ron's afternoons were filled with the sheer joy with which he used his body.

In high school, Kovic joined both the wrestling and track teams, and he eagerly threw himself into the rigorous exercise regimen prescribed by his coaches for success: wind sprints, sit-ups, push-ups, and other calisthenics. By the end of wrestling practice, Kovic and his teammates were left "gasping for air and running into the showers bent over in pain." The same easy assurance that enabled Ron to win the Christmas wrestling tournament one year could be detected in his pole-vaulting technique. He jumped without shoes and remembers vividly the thrill of running down the approach to the jump.

Ron Kovic (white shirt) breaks free from an opponent's hold in a wrestling competition during his senior year of high school. Kovic, a champion wrestler, devoted himself to sports as passionately as he dedicated himself to Catholicism and his country.

Ron could not wait to wear the varsity athletic letter *M*, to win a championship and be loved as a hero at Massapequa High. Such glory brought honor, but it also brought the popularity that might attract the girls of his class. Ron was strong and attractive. He had even heard one pretty freshman declare, "There goes Kovic. He sure is cute." He longed for a girlfriend, or even "someone to hold my hand," but was too shy to act on his desires.

In addition to the physical changes to his body that had come from intensive training, there were other changes happening that he seemed to have no control over. He had entered the world of puberty, of blackheads and new splotches of hair on his face and chest. His body began doing strange things, and he began to explore his sexuality. Kovic came to understand that the changes in his body were a normal part of adolescence, but at the time he felt so much guilt about his feelings for girls that he was too uncomfortable to attend his junior and senior proms.

Ron's high school years had another important role in shaping his view of the world. If the 1950s were known as an era of prosperity in American social life, they were also commonly referred to as an era of "consensus" in American political life. That consensus rested on two basic assumptions. The first of those assumptions, as noted previously, was the myth of abundance, that the United

States had become a "classless" society. Intellectuals of the policy establishment, notably sociologists Seymour Martin Lipset and Daniel Bell, were quick to proclaim the "end of ideology." What they in fact spoke of was the end of socialism in the United States.

In its heyday at the beginning of the 20th century, the Socialist movement offered American workers a way to do battle with the industrial elites who profited from their labors. In 1912, the party boasted 118,000 members, with some 1,200 officials elected to office around the United States.

In the three decades prior to World War II, socialism had gained a sizeable following in the United States with its promise of economic and political equality. The adversity of the Great Depression contributed no small part to this fascination. American workers at the beginning of the 1930s had good reason to wonder whether capitalism had been a great failure. Many American intellectuals began to wonder whether perhaps the socialism practiced by the world's other great superpower, the Soviet Union, could bring greater prosperity to the United States.

During the depression years, large numbers of poets, writers, and artists expressed solidarity with the American Communist party. In the presidential election of 1932, the Communist candidate was chosen by, among others, Ernest Hemingway, Katherine Anne Porter, Richard Wright, Edmund Wilson, Nathaniel West, and Langston Hughes.

But public support for socialism would soon wither. With the consolidation of the American labor movement under the umbrella of the Democratic party, the pact between Hitler and Joseph Stalin of the Soviet Union in 1937, Stalin's barbarous purges during the same decade, the economic boom of the war years, and the rise of anti-Communist hysteria, as practiced by Senator Joseph McCarthy and the House Committee on Un-American Activities, organized socialism in the United States on a large scale had all but disappeared by the mid-1950s. In its place could be found the second basic assumption of the so-called liberal consensus: that the greatest source of danger to the United States, indeed to the world, lay in the spread of Soviet communism.

News of the Communist menace, advancing like Godzilla on the foothills of the Japanese countryside, had not escaped Massapequa. Like many other children in the 1950s, Kovic watched a program called "I Led Three Lives" on television. The show told the story of a double agent who infiltrated the Communist party and reported its activities to the U.S. government. Communists, one read in the newspapers, were out to destroy the way of life that Americans had all sacrificed so much to achieve. Kovic and his friend Richie Castiglia became so obsessed with the supposed threat of Communists that they even began to watch one of their teachers, whom they suspected was secretly a Soviet agent.

Wisconsin Senator Joseph McCarthy made a career out of whipping up anti-Communist hysteria. Often using fraudulent charges, he stimulated the public's fear of Communist "subversion" in order to bully Socialists and liberals by associating them with the so-called Communist threat. In the June 9, 1954, congressional hearing shown below, Army counsel Joseph Welch listens to McCarthy in disgust; he denounced McCarthy that day as a "cruelly reckless character assassin."

A group of draftees are sworn into the U.S. Army on January 10, 1967, in Pennsylvania. Although many soldiers had volunteered, including Ron Kovic, the Vietnam War was fought largely by young men just out of high school who were drafted into the armed forces.

It was in this context that Ron listened, enthralled, when in 1964 two Marine recruiting officers came to speak to the boys of his graduating high school class about joining up. Dressed in crisp blue uniforms and polished black shoes, the two men seemed more like statues. To Kovic, "It was like all the movies and all the books and all the dreams of becoming a hero come true." The two sergeants captured Ron's imagination with their talk of honor, discipline, and patriotic service.

The previous year, President John F. Kennedy had been assassinated in Dallas. Ron had watched television with his parents as the new president, Lyndon Johnson, was sworn in aboard Air Force One. He had seen the alleged assailant, Lee Harvey Oswald, being shot on live television by Jack Ruby. "It all seemed wild and crazy," said Kovic, "like some Texas shootout, but it was real." The Kennedy assassination affected him deeply, as it did most of the country. The 46-year-old president had seemed for all the world like "a dear friend," Kovic remembered.

Kennedy had prodded Ron Kovic's generation to "ask not what your country can do for you," but rather to "ask

what you can do for your country." After listening to the
Marine Corps recruiters in his high school auditorium, Ron
felt prepared to do just that.

> I couldn't wait to run down after them, meet with them
> and shake their hands. And as I shook their hands and
> stared up into their eyes, I couldn't help but feel I was
> shaking hands with John Wayne and Audie Murphy. They
> told us that day that the Marine Corps built men—body,
> mind and spirit. And that we could serve our country like
> the young president had asked us to do.

Kovic was proud of his father, of his daily toil on behalf
of his family. But Ron, who himself worked part-time at
the grocery store, did not wish to spend his life in the
A&P. He had other dreams. One of those dreams—to play
for the New York Yankees—seemed within reach when
Kovic was given the opportunity to try out for the team,
but at the last moment he changed his mind and did not
show up for the trials. There were other heroic visions, of
flying in space or becoming a priest. By the end of high
school, however, all of these goals receded behind the one
that continued to occupy Ron's daily imagination: serving
his country in the struggle to keep communism from
spreading into Vietnam.

Finally, Ron decided to make that dream a reality. In the
summer of 1964, just after graduation, he went down to
the Levittown Marine Corps recruiting station, accompanied by his father. In the red, white, and blue shack, Kovic
declared his intention to join the marines. Ron felt this
decision was nothing less than an obligation he owed his
country. He would serve his country, and, if necessary, he
would die for it. Looking back at that time, Kovic recalls,

> I stayed up most of the night before I left, watching the
> late movie. Then 'The Star-Spangled Banner' played. I
> remember standing up and feeling very patriotic, chills
> running up and down my spine. I put my hand over my
> heart and stood rigid at attention until the screen went
> black.

President Ngo Dinh Diem of South Vietnam gives Colonel McCown of the U.S. Army a tour of the grounds outside his summer home in 1963. That same year, Diem was killed in a military coup; the U.S. government knew of the plans in advance but did nothing to stop them.

3

THE TIME
OF ILLUSION

"THE PRESENT U.S. OBJECTIVE in Vietnam is to avoid humiliation,"
wrote Assistant Secretary of Defense John McNaughton in a March
1965 memo. For McNaughton and the others in the Pentagon and the
foreign-policy establishment, what was at stake was primarily the
United States's reputation as a first-rate military power. But that was
a premise for which the American people were unwilling to risk the
lives of thousands of young men. Thus began a tortuous era in American life, a time of division and, as the journalist Jonathan Schell put it,
"a time of illusion."

Only a few weeks before President Kennedy was shot in Dallas and
Lyndon Johnson was sworn in, the South Vietnamese prime minister,
Ngo Dinh Diem, a fervent anti-Communist, had himself been assassinated when his brutal treatment of Buddhist monks brought him into
disfavor with the South Vietnamese military. President Kennedy had
known of plans for the coup but did nothing to prevent it. By that time,

the United States had 15,000 so-called advisers in South Vietnam. Of course, "advisers" was a somewhat misleading euphemism for troops, some of whom had already engaged in combat.

The United States's interest in Vietnam preceded the Kennedy administration and even the Eisenhower administration before it. As early as 1948, George Kennan, a member of the State Department's policy planning staff, had laid out a policy of "containment," which guided U.S. foreign policy throughout the next three decades. Kennan argued that preventing, or "containing," the spread of Soviet communism ought to be a singularly important goal for the United States as it entered the new cold war era. As later seen in the case of Vietnam, that policy amounted to little more than preserving American "prestige."

As Communist-led governments came into power in China and North Korea, senior officials in the U.S. government feared that these changes threatened American interests in the Far East. In a strange manipulation of logic, the U.S. government became willing to put aside its own democratic principles to counter the perceived threat. As Kennan put it bluntly in a State Department paper, "we should cease to talk about vague and—for the Far East— unreal objectives such as human rights, a raising of living standards, and democratization. The day is not far off when we are going to have to deal in straight power concepts."

This worldview led the United States to throw its support behind Diem at the end of the Vietnam war of independence, when the Viet Minh army of revolutionary leader Ho Chi Minh succeeded in ridding the country of the French, who had brutally ruled Vietnam as a colony for close to a century. The cease-fire negotiated in Geneva, Switzerland, in 1954 divided Vietnam into two separate nations: the North, under the control of the Communists; and the South, under a Catholic minority government led by Diem. Diem had taken power with a rigged election and had rejected subsequent elections called for by the Geneva

The swamps and jungles of Vietnam have been home to a proudly independent people for thousands of years. The Vietnamese fought to maintain their independence from the Chinese for centuries, but were conquered by the French in 1883. The Vietnamese finally rid themselves of the French soldiers in 1954, but the French were quickly replaced by the Americans.

agreement, but the United States chose to back him anyway because of his rigidly anti-Communist views.

The support of the United States for France, and later for the Diem regime, was a blow to North Vietnamese leader Ho Chi Minh. Ironically, Ho's Viet Minh army had been trained by men from the U.S. Office of Special Services, the precursor to the modern-day CIA, during World War II. Ho, schooled in the West and fluent in English, French, and Russian in addition to three Chinese dialects, had even used some of Thomas Jefferson's elegant language in declaring Vietnamese independence in his 1945 address in Hanoi.

Vietnam, settled more than 2,000 years earlier by wandering tribes of both Indian and Chinese descent (hence the regional expression "Indochina"), had led a decidedly independent existence through centuries of rule by a succession of dynasties. The Vietnamese people had throughout their history exhibited a great cultural cohesion and respect for authority. Armed with those two important characteristics, they had successfully repelled repeated attempts by various Chinese ruling families to claim the Vietnamese territory through the ages.

The rise of mercantilism in the West led to the subsequent growth of colonial empires in Europe, on whom the rich history of Vietnam was largely lost. To the French, this far-flung outpost represented first and foremost a

Ho Chi Minh, leader of the Communist-led revolution that liberated Vietnam from the French, had previously traveled in the United States and studied Marxism and literature in Paris, France. When Ho's army won independence for Vietnam in 1954, however, the United States threw its support behind Diem's minority Catholic regime.

source of revenue and trade. In the latter part of the 19th century, the French succeeded in seizing control of the country away from its imperial rulers, and in 1883 Vietnam became a French protectorate. Over the next 50 years, the Vietnamese people were systematically stripped of their political, economic, and human rights.

For the first time, surplus rice that had been saved for the people was traded for export revenue. Kicked off their land, peasant farmers were forced to work in the giant rubber factories built by Michelin and other French companies or in the coal mines that had recently been created. Under strict rule of force, the Vietnamese people were paid a pittance for their labors, and the vast revenue generated by the new export market was returned to the French people, whose own taxes could now be reduced, thus eroding liberal opposition at home for France's colonial project.

The Vietnamese did not accept the French without a fight, and many of the strategies of jungle warfare that would be employed later against the United States were tested first during this period. But without coordination and discipline all of these efforts failed to budge the French. All of these efforts, that is, except for the revolution led by Ho Chi Minh.

Originally named Nguyen Tat Thanh, Ho Chi Minh was born in the central region of Vietnam in 1890. After teaching briefly in a southern village as a young man, he traveled to Saigon. In 1911, he began a 30-year exile after signing on to a French freighter as a galley boy. Over the next decade he would travel to the United States and England before settling in Paris, where he quickly became active in the intellectual circles of the city. He spoke warmly of the work of Victor Hugo and Voltaire, in whose writings he found the "spirit of brotherhood and noble love of peace."

Though Ho might perhaps have wished to lead a simpler life of quiet study and scholarship, he sensed a historic role for himself that could not be ignored. Some 10 years later, after traveling to and from the Far East on many occasions to establish the political framework for a Vietnamese Communist party, Ho would tell a French friend, "I have always thought I would become a scholar or a writer, but I've become a professional revolutionary."

In fact, though Ho was required to engage in a revolution to gain independence from France, his initial goal was for a peaceful transition to democracy in Vietnam. In 1919, as U.S. president Woodrow Wilson arrived at Versailles to sign the treaty ending World War I, Ho sent him a letter that read, in part, "all subject peoples are filled with hope by the prospect that an era of right and justice is opening to them."

Perhaps democracy could have come to Vietnam without the terrible bloodshed and loss of life that resulted from the Communist-led revolt. That would have required a respect for the history, culture, and social institutions of the Vietnamese people that the French did not possess. Instead they fought Ho's forces with determination. In 1954, after nine years of fighting, Ho's army won and declared independence for Vietnam. When the country was divided in Geneva, the United States rejected Ho and threw its support behind Diem.

If France's vision was clouded by its colonial—and one might even say racist—mindset, the United States's own

A combined French and Vietnamese force wades through the mud during an attack on Communist guerrillas in the swampy Mekong Delta, just 40 miles south of Saigon, in May 1954. That same year, the Communist guerrillas successfully ousted the French colonialist government, winning independence for their country after a nine-year war.

relationship with Vietnam owed much to another cloudy perspective that came to be known as the domino theory. The domino theory presumed that the Communist nations of the world moved in a coordinated fashion and that as each new country fell under Communist influence its neighbor was sure to follow. The theory further presumed that the goals of communism were the same in every country in which this ideology had taken root.

The origins of the domino idea can perhaps be best understood in light of the fear generated by the murderous purges of Soviet leader Joseph Stalin during the 1930s and 1940s. Though Ho received no support from the Soviet Union at the beginning of his revolution, and in fact looked to the United States as a model of democratic government, the American determination to "contain" communism around the globe made no room for such historical realities.

After the 1954 Geneva agreement, the United States began stepping up its support for the South Vietnamese government. When the Diem regime refused to comply with the reunification provision of the Geneva agreement (because Diem knew that he could not win a fair election), South Vietnamese Communists carried on their struggle under the umbrella of the National Liberation Front, which became known as the Vietcong. Over the next five years, the Diem regime embarked on a terror campaign to quell the revolutionary activity in the countryside where the Vietcong operated. In the North, overzealous Communist cadres set up Agricultural Reform Tribunals, before whom thousands of innocent farmers were sentenced to death for their alleged assistance to the French regime.

From the Eisenhower administration through the Kennedy administration, U.S. policy operated on the assumption that the Viet Minh forces of Ho were coordinating the efforts of the Vietcong in the civil war against the American-backed government. In fact, however, a Pentagon paper to President Johnson written at the end of 1964

observed that "despite a large and growing North Vietnamese contribution to the Viet Cong insurrection, the primary
sources of Communist strength in the South remain indige-
nous [local]." Just a short time before that, the CIA itself
had refuted the notion of the domino theory responding to
a request for an analysis on the subject from President
Johnson, the CIA's own analysts wrote:

> With the possible exception of Cambodia, it is likely that
> no nation in the area would quickly succumb to commu-
> nism as a result of the fall of Laos and South Vietnam.
> Furthermore a continuation of the spread of communism
> in the area would not be inexorable, and any spread which
> did take place would take time—time in which the total
> situation might change in any number of ways unfavorable
> to the Communist cause.

The United States's entry into Vietnam, as many historians
have observed, was remarkable for the simplemindedness
of the assumptions of the foreign policy establishment.
The U.S. defense "experts" would have needed only to
study the history of Vietnam to understand that the existence of Ho Chi Minh's Communist party owed more to
the centuries-old ties of national identity and political
independence that bound the Vietnamese people together
than to any allegiance to Moscow or Peking. In 1959, one
peasant in South Vietnam told Stanley Karnow, author of
Vietnam, a History (1983), "We are always for the government—no matter which government is in control. But in
our hearts we like the government that takes the least from
the people, and gives them abundance and happiness. We
do not yet have that government."

At their most cynical level, the assumptions of State
Department officials were designed to obscure the United
States's true objectives from the American people. At one
point in 1965, McNaughton went so far as to assign
percentages to the basis for the American presence in
Vietnam:

70%—To avoid a humiliating U.S. defeat (to our reputation as guarantor).
20%—To keep South Vietnam (and then adjacent) territory from Chinese hands.
10%—To permit the people of SVN to enjoy a better, freer way of life.
Also—To emerge from crisis without unacceptable taint from methods used.
Not—To "help a friend," though it would be hard to stay in if asked out.

General William Westmoreland visits the troops in Vietnam. Westmoreland was considered by Norman Schwarzkopf, later the commander of the U.S.–led forces in the 1991–92 Persian Gulf War, to be more concerned with the media and the politicians back home than with the men under his command.

In other cases, the confusion resulted from a reading of events of the previous decade that simply did not add up. British historian Godfrey Hodgson has characterized as "bizarrely unreal" the perspective of State Department officials who somehow seemed to forget that North and South Vietnam had previously been a single country. Writes Hodgson,

> The administration, in its inner debates just as much as in its statements for outside consumption stuck to the rigid notion that a country called South Vietnam was being invaded by its "neighbor," North Vietnam, exactly as if Mexico were being invaded by the United States. This notion contradicted the facts of Vietnamese language, ethnology, politics and history, but it had the simple merit of providing a legal rationale for American intervention.

In practical terms, all of these justifications and misreadings led inexorably to a buildup of U.S. military personnel. In August 1964, President Johnson came before the American public and Congress to announce that U.S. destroyers in the Tonkin Gulf had been fired upon. In response, U.S. planes had targeted a number of North Vietnamese torpedo bases and oil installations. What the American people did not know was that the U.S. ships had been assisting the South Vietnamese in commando raids that were designed to draw North Vietnamese fire, which could be used as a pretext for commencing the air strikes.

It remains unclear even today whether the U.S. ships were in fact ever fired upon, but President Johnson used the incident to win support for his policy and gain authorization from Congress to take "all necessary measures to repel any armed attack against forces of the United States and to prevent further agression." The so-called Tonkin Gulf resolution passed by a vote of 88 to 2 in the U.S. Senate and unanimously in the U.S. House of Representatives. Though it was not a formal declaration of war, the looseness of the resolution's language gave Johnson the flexibility to escalate U.S. participation in the war without the consent of Congress.

After an American barracks in Pleiku, South Vietnam, was shelled by Vietcong soldiers in February 1965, Johnson launched a new air offensive, given the name Operation Rolling Thunder, in which strategic sites in North Vietnam were hit by repeated air strikes. Though in retrospect it now appears that North Vietnam became active in the civil war in the South only after U.S. attacks began, American military commanders acted on the mistaken belief that they could hit the Vietcong at its source. The president couched the operation in language that argued that the United States had "no intent to wage an offensive war," but that clearly was the objective.

By the end of July 1965, the Johnson administration had increased U.S. troop strength in Vietnam to 193,000. Under the command of General William Westmoreland, those troops had seen their role expand from defending the bases out of which air sorties were flown to going out on "search and destroy" missions in a zone just north of Saigon. Before the troops could participate in such activities, they had to be trained at bases in the United States— bases such as Parris Island, South Carolina.

Eager to serve his country and fight communism, Ron Kovic enlisted in the U.S. Marine Corps the summer after he graduated from high school.

4

"This Is My Rifle, This Is My Gun"

WHEN KOVIC ARRIVED at Parris Island he was corralled into formation with the other young recruits, 80 in all. They came from across the country, short and tall, skinny and fat, long haired and short haired. One common thread now tied them together. They had given up their civilian identities to become U.S. Marines, and it fell on Sergeant Mullins and Staff Sergeant Joseph to take them through their basic training.

Ron looked at the two instructors in their shiny black shoes and neat, crisp uniforms with a mixture of awe and terror. "Awright, ladies!" Sergeant Joseph barked at the men, "Your souls today may belong to God, but your asses belong to the United States Marine Corps!" These men whom Ron held in such high esteem began their first day of drills by hurling abuse at the boys.

The recruits goofed their first order, turning to the right as Sergeant Joseph yelled "left face!" Joseph approached one of the boys at random and took out his anger toward the entire group. "You no good f——ing civilian maggot!" he screamed. "You're worthless, do you understand? I'm going to kill you." Of course, generations of army grunts had been treated in the same coarse manner. But Ron did not understand why they had to yell so loudly, with such hate.

With their helmets teetering on their heads and cartridge belts hanging loosely from their waists, Kovic and his companions were led into a large empty hangar and lined up beside a row of empty boxes. They were instructed to take off all of their clothes and place them in the numbered box directly in front of them. As the sergeant put it, "I want you to take off everything that ever reminded you of being a civilian."

As the boys complied, Ron found himself conflicted over what to do with a small medal given to him by his mother, which he wore around his neck. "Can I keep it?" he asked one of the instructors.

"Don't talk back to me," the sergeant responded, throwing the medal unceremoniously into the empty box. "You f——ing maggot. Don't you ever talk back to me!" the man continued. All around Kovic there were men screaming and yelling, and his ears pounded with their words. Sergeant Mullins even punched him as he briefly stepped out of line, and Ron began to wonder whether he really wanted to be there. Perhaps he had made a mistake. All the bullying and tough talk was starting to get to him.

After the boys had stripped they were led to a barbershop, where their hair was cut so quickly and efficiently that it reminded Kovic of sheep being sheared. Next they were thrown into showers. "Wash all that civilian scum off your bodies!" the sergeant shouted. When they returned to the hangar, the boys pulled out their military togs from the boxes into which they had earlier thrown their civilian clothes. None of them had been fitted for a uniform, and so in many cases their boots, shirts, and pants did not fit so well. With a large cap covering part of his face and

U.S. Marine Corps recruits put on their newly issued uniforms during basic training in 1960. Ron Kovic attended boot camp at the age of 18 at Parris Island, South Carolina.

oversize trousers falling below his boots, Kovic himself felt like "a ragamuffin doll."

As the young men dressed, the drill instructors gathered around one boy whose pants were too tight. He was a little overweight, and the other boys watched as the sergeants screamed and laughed at him. Kovic remembered that the same kid had earlier boasted about his own father's heroic exploits during World War II and announced to all who would listen that he was not afraid of anything. Now that the sergeants were poking the boy, noted Ron, "he was just like a little frightened baby."

As the boy started to cry, the sergeants moved in for the kill. "Are those tears?" asked one. "Cry, cry, cry you little baby! That's what we want, we want you people to cry like little babies because that's all you maggots are. You are nothing!" As the heavy boy convulsed in fear on the floor of the hangar, Ron once again wondered what this world had to do with him. Sensitive to the nasty epithets the sergeants were heaping on the sobbing boy nearby, Kovic wished he could go home.

He later found himself thinking that same thought as they marched over to the barracks for their first night on Parris Island. He had seen a few men collapse on the parade deck as they jogged in their heavy equipment to the long wooden building. But he had made it this far, and he could not give up now. Perhaps the humiliation and abuse had a purpose. The men would need to feel a kind of rage if they were to be "successful" soldiers—if they were to kill men, women, and children with whom they had no quarrel. For now, the rigors of basic training served another purpose for Ron. It tested his endurance, his commitment to defeating communism, and, he believed, his manhood.

Instead of receiving even the most general knowledge about the history and culture of the country in which they would soon be asked to risk their lives, Kovic and his fellow soldiers' education took the form of repetitive call-and-response drills and a blur of invective from the training officers. In the three months Ron spent on Parris Island, the words were pounded into him day after day. One day the sergeants would be shouting at him, *"I want you to believe this afternoon that this thing out there is a Commie sonofabitch."* Another day he would have to chant, *"This is my rifle, this is my gun, this is for fighting, this is for fun."* It all ran together until his head swam with his trainers' words: *"Don't stop people keep running people scum scum swine swine there will be no drop-outs today there will be no quitters in my Marine Corps!"*

When the training ended, the new marines were put on a transport plane and flown halfway around the world to the country they had all been taught to hate and fear. Ron had the good fortune on his first tour of duty to avoid heavy fire from the Vietcong. He returned to Massapequa without having killed a single enemy soldier. He had managed to go to Vietnam and return with his image of John Wayne bravado intact.

Away from the battlefront, he maintained the romantic ideal of valor in war. But Ron had not yet had the chance to prove his heroism. Still proud of his role in the war effort and determined to fulfill what he saw as his responsibility to his country, Kovic signed up for a second tour, by which time he had acquired the rank of sergeant. This time, Kovic was certain, he would get his chance to prove himself.

It was only a matter of time before Ron came face to face with the darker side of the war. One evening, while leading a pregnant Vietnamese woman and her child to the protected safety of a dune on the coast of the China Sea, fighting broke out in a nearby hamlet. It was getting dark, and in the craziness and confusion of the shooting, many of Kovic's fellow soldiers began running away from the village toward the ocean.

That was when the boy from Georgia came running up over the side of the dune. From where Ron lay, crouched, it was difficult to tell if the approaching figure was friend or foe. In a split second, he had to make a decision, and he fired his rifle three times at the man running toward him.

By the time he saw what he had done, Kovic was helpless to take back his shot. The corporal just lay there with a slug through his neck, the life pouring out of his young body. It was horrible and irreversible. Kovic kept repeating to himself, "I killed him. He's dead." Suddenly, everything had changed forever. As far as Kovic knew, he had

> murdered his first man, but it wasn't the enemy, it wasn't the one they had all been taught and trained to kill, it wasn't the silhouette at the rifle range he had pumped holes in from five hundred yards, or the German soldiers with plastic machine guns in Sally's Woods. He'd never figured it would ever happen this way. It never did in the movies.

When Ron informed the major in his battalion of the nature of the attack and the death of the boy from Georgia, the senior officer told him to report back the next day. When Kovic returned to the major's bunker, he laid out the details of the previous night's events. He told the major of the pregnant woman; he told him of the men in Kovic's patrol running scared in all directions; he told him of the confusion and the dune. Finally, Ron came to the corporal. "Major," said Ron, struggling to find the strength to speak the words that rested so heavily on his conscience, "I think I might have . . . I think I might have killed the corporal."

"I don't think so," replied the major. "Sometimes it gets very hard out there. I was out a couple of weeks ago and sometimes it's very hard to tell what's happening." Ron felt sure that the man knew exactly what he was trying to tell him. But somehow the major understood something else, too—Ron's terrible guilt—and in his own way was trying to forgive him, or at least give Kovic the chance to forgive himself. According to Kovic, "It was like going to confession when [I] was a kid and the priest said everything was okay." He felt better, but the guilt would never go away completely. The other men still seemed to talk quietly behind his back about what he had done. As time went on, Kovic hoped he might get a chance to make up for his error, however innocent it might have been.

That opportunity came soon—perhaps sooner than Kovic might have expected, when he was asked by the major to lead a scout team that would make forays into enemy territory. The night he was given this new assignment, he wrote in his diary that he was proud to be "serving America in this its most critical hour." He would be putting his life on the line, but that, wrote Kovic, was "what serving your country was supposed to be about."

Kovic was told to lead a patrol of scouts into a nearby hamlet and set up an ambush. He would be accompanied by a supervising lieutenant. They set out at 8:00 P.M. into the rain, their faces smeared black and their uniforms adorned with appropriate camouflage. They made their way through a rice paddy toward a graveyard near the Vietnamese village. Kovic could smell the fires that glowed in the evening just across the way in the villagers' huts.

Day after day, he had seen the townspeople in their small boats heading toward the mouth of the river to catch fish for their evening meal. Others he would see in the rice fields tending to their crop. For the American soldiers, it did not help that the Vietcong often set up camp in civilian areas. It was hard to differentiate between the two sides of the civil war because the North and South Vietnamese were really one people. Trained on Parris Island simply to hate their East Asian foes, the young marines found that once they got to Vietnam their supposed enemies took on a human face and that distinguishing townspeople from the Vietcong could be difficult. Kovic felt at times that it was perhaps more convenient to hate them all, though he tried very hard not to.

General Maxwell Taylor had cautioned against sending additional U.S. troops to Vietnam as early as 1965 precisely because of this vexing matter. Godfrey Hodgson wrote in *America in Our Time* (1976) that Taylor

> warned that what he called "white-faced soldiers" wouldn't be able to tell the difference between friendly and unfriendly Vietnamese; that the marines were neither trained nor equipped for jungle warfare; and that, like the French before them, they would fail at it.

It is in this context that the actions of Kovic's scout team on that fateful evening are perhaps best viewed. The lieutenant and another soldier, Molina, made a preliminary check on the hamlet in the distance. They reported back to Kovic and the other scouts, who were waiting on a dike not far from the cemetery, that they had seen men with rifles moving up ahead. "I think we found them. I think we found them," the senior patrolman whispered when they returned. The rain made it difficult to get a good take on the enemy soldiers' position, and the scouts waded through the rice paddy closer toward them.

The lieutenant then asked Ron to order one of the men to fire a flare over the hamlet to get a better view of the Vietcong. The flare was sent up, lighting the village. The

In 1967, civilian refugees leave with their belongings during a U.S. Marine sweep of the valley in which they live in South Vietnam. Widespread support for the Vietcong among the peasants led U.S. forces to burn or bulldoze entire villages. Kovic himself was involved in a massacre of civilians who were mistaken for enemy soldiers.

enemy soldiers appeared to be concentrated around a fire in one particular hut. In the tension of the moment, one of the scouts tripped the trigger on his gun. Kovic recalls,

> Suddenly someone was firing from the end with his rifle, and now the whole line opened up, roaring their weapons like thunder, pulling their triggers again and again without even thinking, emptying everything they had into the hut in a tremendous stream of bright orange tracers that crisscrossed each other in the night.

When it was all over, they could hear screaming voices from the direction of the hut. No one had given a fire order, and the lieutenant was furious. As they made their way to the hut they could not have been prepared for the enormity of their error. Entering the thatched structure, Molina flashed a light onto the "enemy" wounded. "Oh God," he exclaimed. "Oh Jesus Christ. We just shot up a bunch of kids." Kovic joined him in the hut, only to find a group of children with bullet wounds all over their bodies, their arms and legs shaking uncontrollably.

An old man lay in the corner, his head blown off above his eyes. Kovic described the harrowing sight of the carnage they had wrought.

> A small boy next to the old man was still alive, although he had been shot many times. He was crying softly, lying in a large pool of blood. His small foot had been shot almost completely off and seemed to be hanging by a thread.

In the midst of the screaming children, Ron could not help feeling that he was somehow in a strange, terrible dream. But the feeling was fleeting. He had no time to lose in reverie, and he quickly set to the hopeless task of bandaging the wounds of the Vietnamese boys and girls.

"Where are the rifles?" asked the lieutenant, as villagers from the hamlet began to look in on the bloodied hut. "There aren't any rifles," Kovic responded, still busy tending to the helpless kids. While a soldier with a radio called for a helicopter, the other scouts in Ron's group stood motionless on the floor of the hut, crying in the rain. They could hardly hear their lieutenant's harsh words: "You're men, not babies. It's all a mistake. It wasn't your fault. They got in the way. Don't you people understand—they got in the goddamn way!" But Ron and the other American soldiers knew that it was not true.

Not long after the massacre, Kovic's battalion was hit by an artillery attack. Eleven men died, their flesh torn and mangled like the children he had seen in the Vietnamese hut, like the boy from Georgia he had killed. Kovic started getting anxious to get out of this crazy place. He began taking risks, walking across fields looking for booby traps, hoping that one of them would explode and send him home with a medical discharge. He had not wanted to suffer any permanent injury, just something to get him out of there, out of the confusion and the killing.

This 1967 photograph shows a typical U.S. Marine encampment on the front lines at Con Thien, South Vietnam. Kovic was serving his second tour of duty in Vietnam at the time.

In January 1968, Kovic was pleased to find that the patrols had been terminated, at least for the time being. The men spent their time mending their tent and fortifying the bunker. Then, just as they began to get restless, the body of a lieutenant in the battalion was brought in with a single bullet through the back of his head. He had been involved in some fighting just north of their location, and now the major indicated to Kovic that they would have to move out and head north across the river. The whole battalion felt a certain unease as they stepped into formation.

As they approached the southern bank of a river, the troops ground to a halt. Word had it that the South Vietnamese Popular Forces were being routed in a village on the northern side of the river. An order was relayed to turn back, but soon that order was reversed and the men learned that they were to lead an assault on the village across the river. The plan sounded ill-fated to Kovic and his comrades, and they began to wonder if this day would be their last. Kovic later wrote,

> It all sounded so crazy and simple. I kept trying to get my thoughts together, trying to think how much I wanted to prove to myself that I was a brave man, a good marine. No matter what happened out there, I thought to myself, I

could never retreat. I had to be courageous. Here was my chance to win a medal, here was my chance to fight against the real enemy, to make up for everything that had happened.

As Kovic led a line of men toward the village he was filled with pride. Though only 10 men, they were well armed. The Vietnamese officer from the Popular Forces refused to join them, because in his opinion the attack was doomed. But Kovic was not deterred. From his perspective, the Americans were moving beautifully into position, "just like in the movies." It was not long before the first shots rang out. Kovic and his men began firing at the enemy, but soon it was clear that they were outnumbered. As the other marines fled from their position, Ron held his ground.

As he moved closer toward the village, Kovic took his first hit—in his foot. Falling to the ground, he looked at his heel, now nearly blown off. The pain was terrible. Yet, convinced that there was still an opportunity to play the hero, Ron continued firing. He began limping, and then fell down on his knees. Another soldier ran toward him to apply a bandage to his foot, and just as quickly disappeared into the safety of the tree line behind them. Kovic, determined to redeem himself and become a hero, was the only American still shooting. When his rifle jammed, he paused to clear sand from the chamber. It was then, as he stood to get off the next round of shots, that the bullet hit his right shoulder and tore through his lung, severing his spinal cord.

As Ron felt his body give, he could not tell if he were alive or dead, blown up or intact. Reaching down toward his legs, he could tell that they were still there, but they had no feeling. In fact, his entire body below the chest seemed completely numb. Lying helpless on the ground, Kovic felt torn by conflicting emotions: an unwavering determination that he had not come so far just to die in the sand; the dim hope that he might finally be going home; and fear that if he died it might have all been for nothing.

Within just a matter of minutes Kovic was lifted out of his pit in the sand by a tall black soldier, who risked his life to carry Ron to safety. He could still hear the sound of artillery pounding the troops around him, as other soldiers brought him on a stretcher to a helicopter that had arrived to evacuate the wounded. To his side he could see one man whose intestines seemed literally to be falling out of his body as he did his best to hold them in with his hands. "Oh please, oh no, oh God, oh help! Mother!" the young man was screaming.

From the helicopter, Kovic was transferred to an army medical station. In the ambulance with him on the ride to the makeshift hospital was another soldier whose legs had been blown off during the same battle. Though Ron could barely stand to look at the man, writhing in pain, he somehow envied him as well. "You at least have part of your legs," Kovic told him. When Ron arrived at the hospital, a priest performed the last rites for him. He was

In July 1967, under heavy fire, a group of U.S. Marines carries a wounded comrade from the battlefield to receive medical treatment. When Kovic was wounded in 1968, he was rescued by a fellow marine whose identity he would never discover.

scared that he would die, and the screaming of the other patients only made matters worse.

The overworked doctors seemed to approach their task with a kind of surreal aloofness that frightened Kovic. As they struggled to save the life of one man across the aisle from him, they took bets on an upcoming football game, arguing over the relative strengths and weaknesses of the Green Bay Packers. The soldier died and the doctors moved on to the next patient. All around him, Kovic could feel the shroud of death, suffocating the wounded men. A few beds over, a Green Beret with spinal meningitis cried in vain for his mother. He, too, would die that evening.

Another soldier, his head wrapped in bandages, had been reduced to a near-vegetative state. He was babbling incoherently, and when he urinated into his sheets, a corpsman screamed at him uncomprehendingly. One day a general entered the hospital to award the Purple Heart to the injured men. He walked up and down the aisles, accompanied by a private who took a Polaroid photograph for the men to keep as he gave out their medals. "In the name of the President of the United States, I present you with the Purple Heart," announced the general at each bedside. When he arrived at the bed of the man with the bandaged head, he made the same pronouncement, seemingly oblivious to the man's condition.

After seven days in the hospital, Kovic's condition had improved. His operation was a success, and his shoulder and foot seemed to be healing. Below his chest, his body was still numb, but he was alive. Finally, they came for him, lifted his helpless body into a metal frame, and carried him away from the other broken soldiers. After everything he had seen in Vietnam—the fighting, the wounded men, and the horrors of the medical station—he was going home.

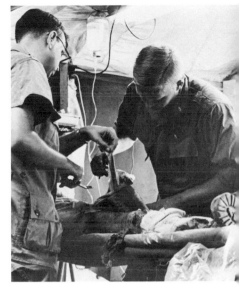

A wounded U.S. Marine undergoes emergency surgery in a portable operating room at a regimental aid station in Vietnam in 1968. Kovic remembers the doctors discussing football as they administered to the injured soldiers.

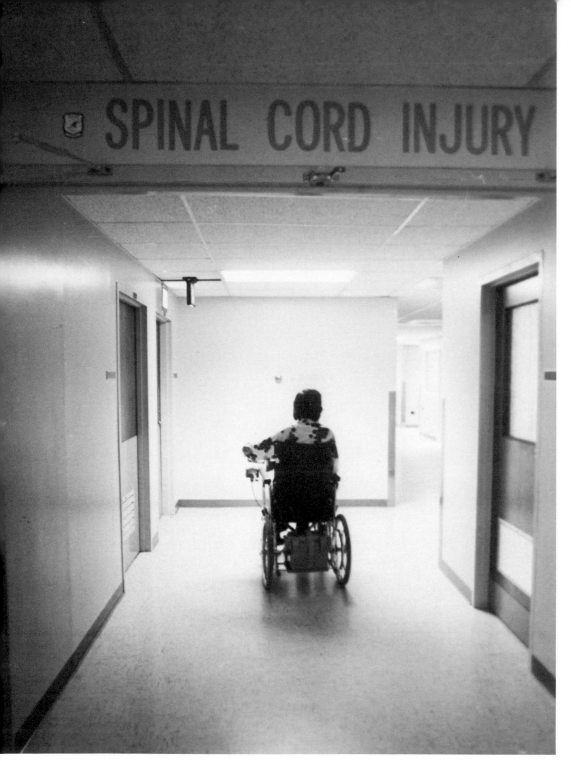

A lone figure wheels down a gloomy corridor in the Spinal Cord Injury ward of a veterans' hospital in Tampa, Florida. Injuries to the spinal cord, which carries messages from the brain to the rest of the body, can make it impossible to feel or move any part of the body below the point of injury.

5

To Hell
in a Hospital

"IT WAS IN THE VA HOSPITALS that I began to first question whether I and the others who had gone had gone for nothing," Ron Kovic declared in 1976 before the assembled delegates at the Democratic convention in New York City. That same week, at a South Street Seaport party for 4,000 supporters of presidential candidate Jimmy Carter, Kovic had grabbed Carter's hand as he made his way through the crowd. Before the governor could pull his hand away, Ron made an urgent plea on behalf of the veterans languishing in hospitals across the country. It was not simply concern for his fellow soldiers that propelled Ron to seize the moment. He spoke from experience.

When Ron Kovic returned from the jungles and beaches of Vietnam it was winter in New York. His first destination was St. Albans Naval Hospital. On the bus ride to the hospital, Ron took great pleasure in breathing in the fresh, cold air. He recalls joking with the other kids on the bus, the "wounded warriors" returning from battle. Kovic felt that he was beginning to "wake up out of the nightmare." Though one nightmare had ended, however, another was just beginning. He was about to come face to face with one of the inexplicable ironies of the U.S. defense bureaucracy: that the financial commitment to armaments and training far surpasses the commitment to healing the men and women who put their lives on the line fighting for their country.

St. Albans was just the first of two hospitals in which Ron would spend the next six months recuperating from his injuries and coming to terms with his new condition. Orderlies from the hospital removed Kovic from the bus in the metal frame that protected him in transit. They brought him to the ward for patients with brain-trauma injuries. Kovic knew he did not belong there. Soon he was transferred to a ward for men with open wounds. His heel had nearly been blown off and required immediate attention.

All around him were stunning reminders of the casualties of war: men blinded by artillery fire; men with no intestines; amputees. Most were about his own age, 21. Kovic noticed the odd expressions on their faces. "They were men who had played with death and cheated it," he thought. Because the men on the ward were still enlisted, reveille was performed each morning at six o'clock, and the men who were able to stood at attention for roll call. The injured soldiers—even the amputees—were expected to clean the ward every day.

With nothing to do, Ron lay on his back during the day remembering what the doctors in Da Nang had told him. He must get used to the idea that he would never walk again. Kovic remembered what a priest had said to him at that time:

> Your fight is just beginning. Sometimes no one will want to hear what you're going through. You are going to have to learn to carry a great burden and most of your learning will be done alone.

Occasionally he had visitors. Men from the Massapequa American Legion dropped by to boost his spirits, but Ron always had the feeling that he was doing the cheering. One morning, a man brought an official-looking envelope to Ron's bedside. Kovic opened it to find that he had been awarded a medal by Governor Nelson Rockefeller for Conspicuous Service to the State of New York. An attached citation was signed by none other than the governor himself.

Ron devoted himself to exercising his upper body whenever he could. Each day he had physical therapy, and he lifted weights to regain his strength. Even so, he could not fail to notice as he sat in the shower that with each passing week, the once-hard muscle tone in his legs was quickly disappearing. In the pain of recognizing the true extent of his frailty, Ron began to feel that his injuries were "the worst he could have received without dying or becoming a vegetable."

Not long afterward, Kovic was transferred to the Bronx veterans' hospital. During the ambulance ride over, his thoughts turned to the beloved Yankees of his childhood, who played not far away in Yankee Stadium. He had skipped his tryout opportunity, but there was now a new finality to his dream of playing on the field where Mantle, Ruth, and DiMaggio had once been heroes.

At St. Albans, Ron had begun to face the challenge of coming to terms with his injury. It had been horrible and painful, but far worse were the new horrors that awaited him in the Bronx. Understaffed, underfunded, and lacking even basic medical supplies, the Bronx hospital seemed to Kovic a living hell on a par with some of what he had seen in Vietnam. With urine bags spilling onto the floor and rats running freely through the wards, the archaic Bronx facility sapped Ron's spirits just at the time he needed optimism and strength above all else.

Across the room from him lay Willey, a young man paralyzed from the neck down. Each morning a nurse came

Upon his return to the United States, Ron Kovic first stayed at this hospital, the St. Albans Naval Hospital in New York, before being transferred to a veterans' hospital in the Bronx. In the poorly maintained Bronx facility (now torn down), the patients fed the numerous rats bread crumbs to discourage them from nibbling on their paralyzed toes.

in to remove fluid from Willey's lungs that had collected during the night. She would remove a cork from the metal attachment to Willey's neck and feed a rubber tube down inside. With a quick slurping sound, the fluid would be sucked into a machine at the side of the bed. The nurse replaced the cork, and it was all over, quick and easy. The procedure seemed incredible to Ron, but the nurse was used to it and completed the task with unnerving nonchalance.

Ron himself felt like "a big, clumsy puppet with all his strings cut." Though he could feel nothing below his chest, in the hospital he learned to hold himself upright in his wheelchair. He quickly managed, through careful twisting and balance, to effect the look of a "normal" man, to cover up the damage that the outside world could never understand and did not want to see. Kovic wrote, "I find it easy to hide from most of them what I am going through."

Every few days each patient was taken to a special room to receive an enema. Because they moved so little in the hospital, their bowels became impacted and had to be relieved. It was at once a fantastic and terrible experience—fantastic for the speed and efficiency with which the process was completed, terrible for the disgusting environment in which it took place. When it was Kovic's turn, he was met at his bed by Tommy, who ran the enema room, and was lifted onto a moving frame to which he would be tied down with bedsheets. Out of a slit at the bottom hung his exposed rear end.

With some 20 patients lined up, Tommy went about his business, feeding soapy water into tanks above the men and fixing the rubber hoses that led down out of the tanks up into their helpless bodies. Some men listened to radios during this process, while others tried to sleep. Tommy ran back and forth between them all with rubber gloves on, attaching and unattaching the hoses, checking their bodies and removing the bedpans when each man had relieved himself.

The waste was emptied into garbage cans, but sometimes it missed and fell on the floor. The men could not go anywhere and had to lie still in the stench of their own waste. A nurse placed the used bedpans into a small steam bath and retrieved them only moments later, clean and sterilized for future use by other patients. To Kovic it was a nightmare. "I want to scream," he thought. "I want to tell them I want out of this. All of this, all these people, this place, these sounds, I want out of this forever."

Following the enema Kovic would be moved to a nearby shower. Another orderly would squeeze liquid soap out of a green plastic container and clean Ron from head to toe, which made him feel as if he were in a car wash, and afterward he would be examined once again by Tommy. It was no mean feat to put 20 men through this regimen each morning. As harrowing and dehumanizing as Kovic found the experience, he remembers with some respect that throughout it all, "Tommy [was] a master."

As time went on, Kovic became more despondent about his condition. Although the injury had seemed interesting to him at first, and somehow tinged with the adventure of war, that feeling did not last long. He did what he could to become stronger. He worked at the parallel bars in the training room and continued to lift weights, heaving the 25-pound bars up and down until his shoulders ached. But all the while he could not escape the reality of his situation, and that of the other men around him.

For Kovic, the most difficult adjustment was only beginning to reveal itself. When he saw some of the women volunteers in the hospital, or when he met the pretty daughters of some of the older men, he began to face another crushing truth about his injury: he no longer had any feeling in, or control over, his penis. Forced to urinate through a rubber catheter, this new circumstance seemed particularly cruel. How could he express his sexuality? What woman would find him attractive now, with his tubing and his impotence?

Ron would later find that sexual satisfaction and romantic love were both still within his reach, but for now all he knew was that he could never have children of his own. All the healing that his body was capable of had already taken place, and to Kovic that was deeply discouraging.

"Now I am left with the corpse, the living dead man, the man with the numb legs, the man in the wheelchair," he lamented. He thought that he would go crazy, or that he had perhaps gone crazy already. While the hospital aides played poker on the toilet bowls of the enema room, down the hall Kovic and his fellow patients suffered the torments of daily life in the ward. The men threw bread crumbs at the rats on the floor by the radiators. From across the room another patient, Briggs, called out with a laugh, "It's a lot better than having the [rats] nibble at your toes during the night." Between the men who smelled for want of proper bathing and others whose sheets had not been changed, Ron could not understand what had happened to them all. "It never makes any sense to us," he thought, "how the government can keep asking money for weapons and leave us lying in our own filth."

From time to time, Ron's family would visit him in the hospital. Kovic's mother brought him a copy of *Sunrise at Campobello* (1959), which described former president Franklin Roosevelt's own battle with polio and his subsequent rise in politics despite his disability. Ron could not bring himself to reveal his true feelings, to tell them what was happening to him: the enema room, the rats, the tube in his penis. Instead he focused on other things, pleasant things, "the things they want to hear." But even Kovic could not protect his family completely from the reality of his life in the hospital.

On one occasion his mother and sister came to see him while he tried out some new braces in the therapy room. Despite his best efforts to keep himself up between the parallel bars, Ron shook as he moved himself forward. His mother and sister watched from a distance in fear, holding

A wounded veteran receives physical therapy at the Bronx veterans' hospital in 1964.

hands and trying to mask with faint smiles the pain and worry etched on their faces.

Jimmy, Kovic's physical therapist, seemed oblivious to the awkwardness of the scene as Ron's pants fell down below his waist. No sooner had Jimmy proclaimed Kovic's success, saying "See, he's standing," than Ron began to throw up all over himself and onto the floor. Thinking of his mother, Ron had told himself earlier, "there are things that I am going through here that I know she will never understand." Perhaps she was beginning to now, if only just a little.

A yard outside the hospital offered Ron a respite from the craziness inside. He liked the green grass and fresh air. He felt certain that the old men sitting out there with him were themselves veterans of World War I. The "war to end all wars," as that conflict was known, had only been followed by more fighting. In the prime of his youth, Kovic sat in a wheelchair, trying to sort it all out. He would read about the progress of the Vietnam War in the newspaper. He would tell those who asked him that the U.S. soldiers were in good spirits. But slowly, Kovic began to have some misgivings. He remembers thinking, "I want things to be simple again, things are too confusing."

Soon Kovic would return to Massapequa, leaving the horrors of the hospital behind. He would be free of the rats and soiled bed sheets, the enema room, the crying in the night. But the confusion? The confusion was only beginning.

Massapequa residents enjoy the annual Memorial Day parade. As a child, Ron Kovic marched with the Cub Scouts in Massapequa, New York, his hometown on Long Island. Years later, as a paralyzed Vietnam veteran, he would serve as grand marshal in the Memorial Day parade there.

6

COMING HOME

RON KOVIC CAME HOME from the hospital in time for his 22nd birth-day, in time for the Fourth of July. His father had already built a ramp into the house so that Ron could come and go as he pleased. It was a good, strong ramp, and his father had put a lot of work into it. He had painted it red so that it blended in with the rest of the house. Looking at it, Ron thought of his childhood, and helping his dad repair the roof. "He was a big hurricane," Kovic wrote of his father. "It seemed important to be moving whenever he was around and acting busy if you didn't have anything to do. He was always moving his big, strong arms." Those arms had now made it possible for Ron to have his freedom. It was the work of a craftsman. It was a work of love.

He remembered, too, the Fourth of July celebrations of his child-hood, the parades down Massapequa Avenue, with the streamers flying and the firecrackers popping. He remembered walking the same route in the Memorial Day parade with his Cub Scout troop, waving to his proud mother on the sidewalk as she watched the procession pass by. This year things were different. The parade would honor him and Eddie Dugan, another Massapequa boy who had lost both of his legs in Vietnam.

When two men from the Massapequa American Legion came by to pick him up, Ron could not help feeling strangely ambivalent about his role in the parade. He and Eddie were to be the grand marshals, and they would occupy the honored position in the convertible at the head of the parade. But somehow, Kovic believed, these people did not understand what he had been through. They tried, but even their compliments sounded hollow to him. "This kid of yours sure has a lot of guts," the tall commander had told his father.

"We're really proud of him," said the other man. "He's sacrificed a lot."

Ron had only begun to question whether that sacrifice had been worth all of this. He felt confused by it all. As

Parades were a focal point of the patriotic culture of Ron Kovic's youth. Returning to Long Island as a paraplegic veteran, Kovic felt alienated and misunderstood by the organizers of the Memorial Day parade, who used him as a symbol but did not allow him to speak to the crowd.

the convertible made its way down the parade route that afternoon, something seemed wrong. Parade volunteers had adorned the car with colorful signs to let the audience know to whom they were waving. WELCOME HOME RON KOVIC AND EDDIE DUGAN, read one. OUR WOUNDED VIET-NAM VETS . . . EDDIE DUGAN AND RON KOVIC, read another. But no one waved. No one approached the car with flower garlands to congratulate their boys, home from war. They just stared.

This was not the hero's welcome Kovic had dreamed of. This was not the reception veterans of other wars had received, the way he had seen it portrayed in the movies. What had happened? wondered Ron. After the parade, volunteers lifted him onto a speaker's platform to listen to the speeches from the mayor, the American Legion commander who had picked him up at home, and others. The commander gave a rousing address on behalf of the cause in Vietnam. With tears in his eyes, he concluded, pointing at Ron and Eddie, "We must win because of them." With hundreds of faces looking at his broken body, Ron felt sick.

It seemed that everyone had something to say about their experience except the two men who had lived it. Ron and Eddie were not even given a chance to speak. Kovic felt like an oddity, like one of the freaks in the circus, being manipulated for the curiosity of others.

When the festivities ended and Ron had been carried from the stage back down to the ground, he heard his name being called in the distance. It was Tommy Law, a child-hood friend, who had himself been injured in a cease-fire zone during the war. Seeing Tommy changed everything. Kovic found himself completely overcome by his emotions. The two men embraced and cried openly in each other's arms. Finally, here was something real that he could hang on to after the patriotic posturing that marked the day's previous events. Here was someone who knew what he was feeling, who had been there, in Vietnam; someone to whom his injuries were not just the stuff of speeches but part of a wrenching and deeply disturbing shared experience.

Part of Tommy's skull had been cracked open during the war and replaced with a metal plate. Tommy did not want to discuss it. Instead he and Ron spent the rest of that afternoon talking over old times. When it got late, Tommy wheeled Ron home through the town where they had grown up together, past the old baseball field, down Hamilton Avenue where they had played with Richie and Bobby and the other kids. All the old places still looked the same as they always had, but for Ron and Tommy everything was different. They had entered the war as wide-eyed boys and returned as damaged men. They had seen and done things that they did not want to remember.

For a while Ron did everything he could to forget. At Arthur's Bar he attempted to drink away the pain. The finality of his injury tormented him. It was not simply the reality of his immobility, the knowledge that he would never walk or run again. Increasingly, Kovic began to feel that his injury had robbed him of his manhood. He saw the pretty women in Arthur's, and he wanted to dance with them. Ron became more and more self-destructive, drinking with his friends to block out his depression.

Lost in despair, Kovic turned to the same inspiration he had turned to as a boy—Jesus. Dipping his hand into the holy water by the crucifix in the family room, he prayed for strength, he prayed for healing, and he prayed for loving. Sometimes he tried writing about his sorrow, typing furiously into the night.

> there was a soldier
> tapdancing softly in the rain
> above the coffin
> six feet above, the people praying

Although words could give shape to what Ron was feeling and somehow heal his mind, they could not heal his body. The drinking continued, and after coming home too drunk

This scene from the movie Born on the Fourth of July *shows Ron Kovic, played by Tom Cruise, in the Mexican desert. Kovic's trip to Las Fuentes provided a temporary respite from loneliness, but there was no escape from the finality of his injury.*

to put himself to bed one evening, Kovic knew something had to change.

If traditional expressions of masculinity were no longer available to Ron, he would have to find a different outlet for his feelings. Soon an opportunity arose—an opportunity that also gave him the chance to leave home for the first time since he had returned from the hospital. Ron had heard of a town in Mexico, Las Fuentes, where there were women who were kind to men like him, women who would not be scared away by his body; where he could reconnect with a part of himself that he had lost; where he felt he might rediscover his sexuality and become a whole man again.

Kovic spent the summer of 1969 in Las Fuentes in a small hamlet called the Village of the Sun. He found a large community of U.S. veterans there. They played cards and swapped war stories through the day and long into the night. There were always lots of women circulating among them. Ron enjoyed exploring the town, its chapel and other points of historic interest. Finally, he attempted his first encounter with a woman. Sadly, in spite of the stories he had heard, it ended abruptly when she was frightened to tears by the sight of his injuries.

Shortly thereafter, however, Ron met a woman who accepted his condition and gave him the loving he had been longing for. She was much more relaxed than the first woman had been. Gentle and kind, she laughed with Kovic as they kissed and held each other under the blankets. She said she had a little girl and that, like Ron, she was lonely. She told him that she had only turned to prostitution to make enough money to support herself and her child. When the woman suggested that they get married, Ron was receptive at first, but then he decided that she had not really meant it. He spent the next evening with another woman.

In time, Ron realized that his life had not really changed in the Village of the Sun. There was as much misunderstanding in Las Fuentes as there had been in Massapequa. On one occasion, a local prostitute had made fun of a friend of Kovic's, Charlie. In a rage, Charlie had thrown a tantrum in the cantina. "They [the U.S. government] made me kill babies!" he kept saying. "They made me kill babies!" Ron shared Charlie's anger, and they were both thrown out of the establishment. In the cab on their way back to the hotel, Charlie carried on to such an extent that the driver stopped and kicked them both out of the car, wheelchairs and all. Soon a truck picked up Charlie and Ron and took them to their destination. By then, Kovic had had his fill of Las Fuentes. He was ready to go home again.

Returning to Long Island, Ron decided that he had already spent too much time living with his family, and, having tasted a bit of independence in Mexico, he realized that the time had come to find his own apartment. Money was not an issue. The checks he received from the government covered the costs of rent and buying new furniture with plenty to spare. Ron had already gained some measure of mobility when he had his car specially fitted so that he could drive without the use of his feet. He found an apartment in Hempstead, Long Island, and moved in.

Though Ron gained a measure of privacy and the opportunity to be self-sufficient, living by himself only increased his isolation and loneliness. When his thoughts turned obsessively to the dead corporal and he began driving at crazy speeds down the highway, Ron looked for a new distraction. He signed up for some college courses and was suddenly surrounded by people again. He also began to practice with leg braces again, allowing himself to hope that he might actually learn to walk.

One day, while stretching his legs, Kovic heard a loud crack. He fell to the floor. When he looked down at his twisted right leg, he saw that the shattered thigh bone had cut right through the surface of his skin. The horror of that moment could not have been greater, for injury meant a return to the Bronx veterans' hospital. Kovic would be hospitalized there for the next six months.

This visit was even worse than the last. Not only had Ron tasted the sweetness of life on his own, but somehow the hospital had become even more menacing and dehumanizing than before. Within the first month, the hospital staff isolated Kovic in a room for poor behavior. His punishment arose from a series of "impertinent" requests he had made. Kovic recalled in his book *Born on the Fourth of July,* "I had a fight with the head nurse on the ward. I asked for a bath. I asked for the vomit to be wiped up from the floor. I asked to be treated like a human being."

Another nurse often fed Ron extra doses of a drug to make him drowsy. The orderlies called him by his room number, Seventeen. Frequently, they would not respond to his call button at all. Lying in his own excrement one afternoon, Kovic rang over and over again for assistance but got no response. Frustrated, he threw an ice pitcher into the hallway. "I'm a Vietnam veteran!" he shouted in pain to anyone who might be listening. Finally an aide came by and heard his screaming. "Vietnam don't mean nothin' to me or any of these other people," he told Kovic. "You can take your Vietnam and shove it up your ass."

Kovic's doctor rarely came by to check his patient, and when he did it was to ask Ron whether he might, in fact, be better off without his leg. He made the procedure sound quick and simple. Kovic thought in horror,

> This place is more like a factory to break people than to mend them and put them back together again. I don't want them to cut my leg off. It is numb and dead but it still means something to me. It is still mine. It is a part of me and I am not going to give it away that easily.

After the doctors operated on Kovic's leg, it looked at one point as if he might not have much choice. He woke up in the hospital's intensive care unit. The surgeon had replaced some of Kovic's shattered bone with a metal plate and attached a special pump to remove fluid from his wound. One tube carried clear fluid into his leg, and another carried red fluid out. The pump kept the whole process flowing.

One day, quite suddenly, the pump stopped. Ron became terrified that he would lose his leg after all. A

Nursing assistant Helena Adams and corrective therapist Frank Albanese (right) assist in a patient's rehabilitation in a Maryland veterans' hospital in 1971. Kovic was himself forced to return to the Bronx veterans' hospital for a six-month stay in 1969 after snapping a leg bone during his own attempted rehabilitation.

hospital aide kicked the machine hard, but nothing happened. "Old equipment," he shrugged, before running to find a doctor. The doctor, an intern from one of the local universities, finally arrived to inform Ron that the pump would probably not start up again. Frantic, Kovic responded, "I can't believe that a modern veterans hospital like this doesn't have an extra pump." The doctor sheepishly told Ron that it was the only pump they had. "The government is not giving us money for things that we need," he added. "It's really too bad. It's not fair at all."

Kovic pleaded, "I've tried so hard to keep this leg . . . I've done everything." The doctor nodded in sympathy, saying "I understand." Of course he could not even begin to understand the anguish Ron was feeling at that moment. But through it all his determination not to give up paid off. An hour later the pump started again for no apparent reason.

As Kovic's leg healed, he began a new period of soul searching. His experience in the veterans' hospital and his disillusionment over his injuries led him to reconsider the message of the protest movement he had been reading about. Since he had returned to the United States, Ron had denounced the protesters as unpatriotic, as un-American. But he had seen with his own eyes what was happening in Vietnam. He had killed innocent women and children. He had even killed one of his own men. And he had seen how the government treated the men who had been asked to give their lives and had returned from the war shell-shocked and crippled.

Another war was being waged on a new battlefront—the war to end the war. It was a war that had no guns, a war comprised of armies of students and other Americans bearing a message of peace. "There's a battle outside and it's raging," sang the poet-folksinger Bob Dylan. "It'll soon shake your windows and rattle your walls." Only a year before, Ron had scoffed at that battle, but now he was beginning to think that perhaps it was time to join up.

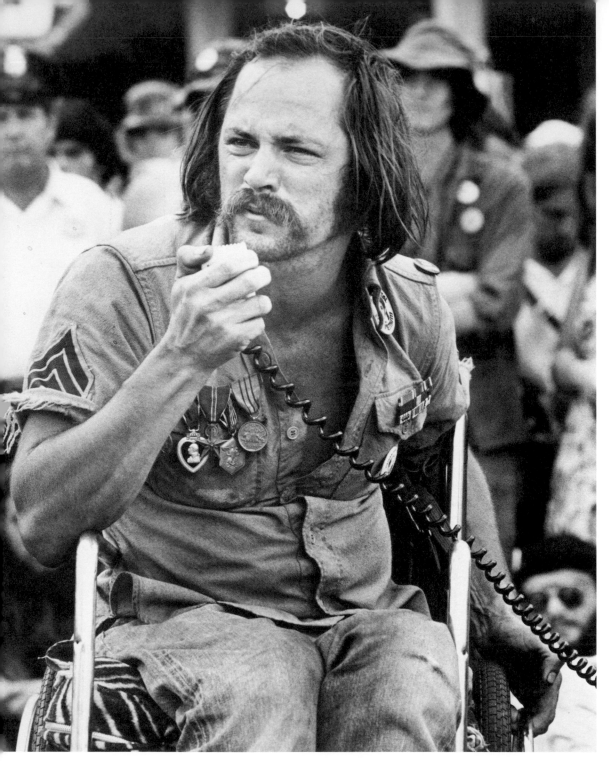

In 1970, Ron Kovic finally found in political activism an outlet for his long-simmering anger regarding his injuries, his treatment in the veterans' hospital, and his growing awareness that the rationale for his patriotic sacrifice had been based on lies.

7

THE OTHER WAR

IN THE SPRING OF 1970, Ron returned to college just as the protests against the Vietnam War started heating up. He remembered how he had felt when he had first heard of the protesters while he was in Vietnam. Then, he had not been able to understand how the demonstrators, most of them young students, could condemn the American soldiers when they were halfway across the world risking their lives. "How could they do this to us?" he had thought at the time. "Many of us would not be coming back and many others would be wounded or maimed. We swore they would pay, the hippies and draftcard burners. They would pay if we ever ran into them." Many returning veterans still felt that way. But after everything Kovic had been through, he had begun to change his mind.

If the country had found the rationale for a U.S. presence in Vietnam compelling at the beginning of 1965, it had become deeply divided by 1968. So divided, in fact, that Johnson had to withdraw from the presidential race that year. Johnson's vice-president, Hubert Humphrey, won the Democratic nomination only after John Kennedy's brother, Robert, a vocal critic of the handling of the war, had been assassinated on the night of the California primary. Humphrey went on to lose to Richard Nixon in the general election. President Nixon did nothing to de-escalate the war over the next year, and as television brought home the grim reality of what American boys were suffering in Vietnam, the tide of public opinion began to shift against the war.

Now it was 1970. In school, Ron kept his distance from the antiwar movement at first. He threw himself into his work, trying not to think too much about the war and the demonstrations. Then it happened. After President Nixon announced the hitherto secret bombing of neutral Cambodia in April, demonstrations erupted on campuses across the country. A national student strike was organized by

On May 7, 1970, members of the National Guard fired bullets and tear gas into a crowd of about 500 students demonstrating against the Vietnam War at Kent State University, killing four and wounding several others. The incident shocked Kovic and drove him into the antiwar movement.

student representatives at Yale University on May 2. On May 4, students at Kent State University, in Ohio, burned down a building used by the Reserve Officers Training Corps (ROTC). The Ohio National Guard was called in and, responding to taunts from students, fired their rifles into the crowd. Four students were killed.

At that point, Todd Gitlin wrote in his book *The Sixties* (1987), "The dam broke. Strikes broke out at about thirty percent of the nation's twenty-five hundred campuses, demonstrations at more than half. . . . Probably between 50 and 60 percent of the students in the United States took part."

Kovic heard the news of the Kent State killings on the radio in his apartment, and "for a moment there was a shock through my body. I felt like crying." He knew then that he had to get involved, and he quickly joined a throng of students who had gathered to voice their anger. There was a great intensity to the reaction on campus, and Kovic decided to participate in a demonstration in Washington on May 9, the following Saturday. He contacted his cousin Ginny's husband, Skip, who had been active in the antiwar effort, and together they made the trek down to the nation's capital.

When they arrived, Ron found a feeling of great camaraderie in the gathering of young protesters, a tremendous sense of sharing and community, as they vented their collective anger at the actions their government was taking in their name in Southeast Asia. He was surprised to find the front of the White House blocked by rows of buses, some 30 or 40 in all, and he could not help wondering, "was the government so afraid of its own people that it needed such a gigantic barricade?" On the grass beside the White House, people were handing out pamphlets indicating that the rally was to be nonviolent.

Amid the speeches and pronouncements, a number of people took off their clothes and cooled themselves in the reflecting pool in front of the Lincoln Memorial. Kovic experienced the moment as a spontaneous expression of

As the death toll mounted in Vietnam, demonstrations like this one in front of the Pentagon in November 1967 became regular occurrences in Washington, D.C. Kovic attended his first mass protest in Washington on May 9, 1970, after the Kent State killings.

freedom, but one tinged with pain; confined to his wheel-chair, he could not participate.

But if the protesters intended to keep the demonstration peaceful, the Washington police had made no such promise. As the day's events wrapped up and the crowd of more than 100,000 prepared to leave, cops entered the crowd on horseback, wielding their clubs and charging at the demonstrators. They shot tear gas into the throng, and a number of people were injured.

It was only the first of many such encounters Ron would have in the next few years, but it left a very lasting impression. Kovic explains,

> The demonstration had stirred something in my mind that would be there from now on. It was so very different from boot camp and fighting in the war. There was a together-

ness just as there had been in Vietnam, but it was a togetherness of a different kind of people and for a much different reason. In the war we were killing and maiming people. In Washington on that Saturday afternoon in May we were trying to heal them and set them free.

Not long afterward Kovic joined a friend of his from the veterans' hospital, Bobby Muller, in speaking engagements at New York area high schools. Ron was acutely aware of the irony. Only seven short years after the two impressive Marine Corps recruiters had visited Massapequa High School with their stories of patriotism, war, and valor, Kovic now sat before another audience of impressionable students with a very different story to tell. The more speaking engagements he made, the less interested he became in college. When his friend Kenny returned from California at Christmas, he asked Kovic if he would be interested in driving back to the West Coast with him. Already frustrated at having to maneuver his wheel-rough the ice and snow, Kovic wasted no time making up his mind. He cleaned out his apartment in a single afternoon, and the following morning they were on the road.

It was not long after they arrived in California and found a new apartment on the ocean that Ron's mind drifted back to the antiwar effort. He was out by the pool of the Santa Monica Day Club when he learned of a large demonstration of Vietnam veterans in Washington, at which many of the men had thrown away their medals to protest the war. Ron immediately decided to look up the local chapter of the Vietnam Veterans Against the War (VVAW) and to go to their next meeting.

Connecting with the VVAW had a profound impact on him. He felt a closer tie to these men than to anyone he had met at the hospital, in Massapequa, or at college. As Kovic put it,

> We were men who had gone to war. Each of us had his story to tell, his own nightmare. Each of us had been made cold by this thing. We wore ribbons and uniforms. We

talked of death and atrocity to each other with unaccustomed gentleness.

It was not long before Kovic was making speeches on behalf of the VVAW. At one rally, actor Donald Sutherland read from a book entitled *Johnny Got His Gun* (1939), by Dalton Trumbo, which told the story of a young American soldier who was literally blown to pieces during World War I and returned home an invalid, pitied, misunderstood, and robbed of the simplest pleasures of a "normal" existence.

Listening, Kovic was moved to tears. He approached the rally organizers and asked if he could read a poem he had written. Though it was against the protocol for the afternoon, they made an exception and let him speak. Ron's words enraptured the audience. Afterward, he was besieged with requests for other speaking engagements. He began to feel that this was what his life had been leading toward. It meant more to him than any of his previous pursuits as an athlete or a soldier. "I think I honestly believed," wrote Kovic, "that if only I could speak out to enough people I could stop the war by myself. I honestly believed people would listen to me because of who I was, a wounded American veteran."

Some of Ron's friends thought he had gone too far, that he had become so wrapped up in his antiwar efforts that the publicity had gone to his head. Kenny, for one, had had enough. He packed his stuff and moved back to New York. For Kovic, though, his new identity had taken on the importance of a crusade. Picketing in front of the Nixon campaign headquarters in Los Angeles, Ron wheeled his chair out into traffic and screamed, "Take a good look at the war!" at the passing motorists.

There was no doubt that Kovic was in the thick of things, and if his friends had stopped paying attention to his efforts, the police certainly had not. The Nixon administration, it is now known, had been extremely paranoid about the activities of the antiwar activists and had gone to great lengths to infiltrate such organizations as the Students for a Democratic Society (SDS) to attempt to turn various factions against each other. The California authorities were no less willing to use harsh measures to subvert the peace movement. Ronald Reagan, the governor at the time, had said himself, "If it takes a bloodbath, let's get it over with."

As one rally in front of the Nixon office intensified, Kovic was approached by a man he had seen at other rallies. "How are you doing, brother?" the man asked. "You look like you could use some help." As the red-haired man began pushing Kovic, police began moving in on the demonstrators. Screaming at his fellow protesters to stay in line, Kovic pushed on the wheels of his chair, but it would not budge. It was then that he realized that the red-haired "brother" was an undercover police officer. "You're under arrest," the man told him.

Before he knew it, Kovic had been pushed out of his chair and onto the ground for handcuffing. He screamed that he was paralyzed, but no one seemed to care. The police continued beating and bloodying the protesters, including Kovic. The cops then threw him into the back-seat of a car and took him down to the station. Only then did they begin to understand what they had just done to him. The sight of his ugly scars and limp, deformed limbs finally made them halt their brutal treatment.

Even so, Kovic was booked and held until someone came down to post his bail. When the booking officer asked his profession, Ron answered, "I'm a Vietnam veteran against the war." The officer, barely able to contain his rage, responded, "You should have died over there." Then, turning to another officer, he added, "I'd like to take this guy and throw him off the roof." Kovic's trust in his government had taken another severe blow, but even worse, he knew he could no longer trust all of his "brothers" in the VVAW. Looking at the other veterans who had been arrested, he wondered, "Which one is the informer now?"

Not long afterward, Kovic met a woman named Helen after one of his speeches at a church. She had been married once and had two kids. They hit it off, but when she quickly declared her love to him, he got scared and flew to New York to see his family for a month or two. Desperately lonely and troubled almost every night by dreams about the dead corporal, he called Helen and asked her to fly back East to join him. He even proposed to her; but the two barely knew each other, and after a brief period of counseling following his return to California, Kovic decided that what he really needed was to be alone. Thus began a period of quiet contemplation. He found a small house near the ocean in Santa Monica, bought a rolltop desk, and started writing. But he was unable to escape his depression.

He had tried hard to overcome the reality of his paralysis, but now it was pulling him down like a leaden weight, sapping his energy and his enthusiasm for life. Sure, others could act as if they understood what he had gone through—what he was still going through—but for Ron the knowledge was always there. The reality of the rubber tube in his penis. The reality of removing the hardened bowel movements from his rectum with a glove each morning. His life *was* more difficult than other people's, and that awful truth soured him. Kovic wrote of his mood during this period,

> All he had tried to do was tell the truth about the war. But now he just wanted it to be quiet, to be where they weren't cursing at him, lying and calling him a traitor. He had never been anything but a thing to them, a thing to put a uniform on and train to kill, a young thing to run through the meatgrinder, a cheap small nothing to make mincemeat out of.

If his anger and self-pity were understandable, they nevertheless had taken Kovic to a place he wanted desperately to get out of: a lonely, friendless place where he felt like a mere dot. But before he could do that he would have to confront the depth of the betrayal he felt. He saw the men who ran the war as hucksters at a county fair, smooth talkers who hid their true ignorance behind words. The defense strategists from the elite colleges of the nation who sent young men off to war—what did they know?

> They had never seen blood and guts and heads and arms. They had never picked up the shattered legs of children and watched the blood drip into the sand below their feet. It was they who were the little dots, the small cheap things, not him and the others they had sent to do their killing.

Even with all the rage inside of him, Kovic searched inside himself for the strength to put his life back on track. He found that strength in the summer of 1972. Kovic joined a long caravan of Vietnam veterans who were driving to Miami, where the Republican party would be staging its national convention. The protesters had a message for President Nixon, who would accept his party's nomination for another term in office. They had formed an army of peace, and they were coming to tell the people of the nation that the war was wrong, that it reaped great profits for the arms manufacturers but left thousands of American boys wounded and neglected.

As the caravan of veterans moved across the country, they were greeted with friendly smiles and cheers from people on the side of the road, from young children and others waving the familiar peace sign. After 1,000 miles, they made their way into the city of Miami. They did not pause for red lights but came rattling through with their horns honking and flags waving, until they reached their destination at Flamingo Park, near the convention site. Well-wishers welcomed them to a giant tent city, and Kovic remembers that the mood was festive as they set up camp for the first night.

If the veterans' camp was brimming with excitement, it was certainly matched by the mood inside the Convention Center in the days ahead. On the night President Nixon was to give his acceptance speech, the Republican party faithful were dressed in their finest suits and elegant dresses. To Kovic they looked "like they were going to a banquet." Kovic entered the hall with a friend who had a press pass and made his way toward the speakers' platform up at the front.

Suddenly he was stopped by a convention official and told he could not go any farther. Soon two other marshals joined them, asking Ron to leave. Kovic spun around in his chair to confront the three men. "I'm a Vietnam veteran and I fought in the war!" he screamed. "Did you fight in the war?" As they looked at him in shock, he continued, "I've got just as much right to be up front here as any of these delegates. I fought for that right and I was born on the Fourth of July."

The officials relented, lest he create a greater scene. They told Kovic he could stay where he was if he promised not to go any farther forward, and Ron consented. He began speaking to those around him about the long caravan

Bill Wieman (left), a friend of Kovic's who lost both his legs in Vietnam, camps with other veterans in East Potomac Park before a demonstration in Washington in 1971. Wieman joined Kovic at the 1972 Republican National Convention in Miami, where the VVAW attempted to disrupt President Nixon's nominating celebration.

of veterans from across the country. His voice grew louder as he described the veterans' hospitals, where men waited for hours in their own excrement for attendants to help them. "And they never come," Ron continued.

> They never come because that man that's going to accept the nomination tonight has been lying to all of us and spending the money on war that should be spent on healing and helping the wounded. That's the biggest lie and hypocrisy of all—that we had to go over there and fight and get crippled and come home to a government and leaders who could care less about the same boys they sent over.

By now, Kovic was creating quite a stir. When another convention official came and asked him to leave, Ron threatened to make such a racket that the television networks would see them beating up a wounded veteran. But he need not have threatened, for Roger Mudd of CBS News was already on his way over.

"Why are you here tonight?" Mudd asked him. The words just poured out of Ron's mouth. Finally, here was an opportunity to reach the American people in one great moment.

> I gave America my all and the leaders of this government threw me and the others away to rot in their V.A. hospitals. What's happening in Vietnam is a crime against humanity, and I just want the American people to know that we have come all the way across this country, sleeping on the ground and in the rain, to let the American people see for themselves the men who fought their war and have come home to oppose it. If you can't believe the veteran who fought the war and was wounded in the war, who can you believe?

Mudd thanked him for his words, and Kovic was pushed by another veteran back to an aisle directly in line with the speakers' platform, where two other veterans, Bobby Muller and Bill Wieman, were parked in their chairs. He joined them, and the three men sat in their wheelchairs with their "stop the war" signs and waited for the moment President Nixon would speak.

Finally, Nixon walked onto the platform to the screaming cheers of the convention. Kovic felt it must have been
the largest ovation the man had ever received. Together,
the three veterans raised their voices. "Stop the war," they
screamed at the president. "Stop the war, stop the bombing, stop the war!" Others in the audience began to shout
them down with more chants of "four more years," as
Secret Service agents made their way to where the men
were yelling. Other agents tried to hide the men from the
view of the president. Finally they were grabbed and
unceremoniously pushed out of the hall. As they exited one
man spat in Kovic's face and called him a traitor. The rage

kept pouring out of Kovic. "I served two tours of duty in Vietnam!" he told one newsman. "I gave three-quarters of my body for America. And what do I get? Spit in the face!"

Soon, Ron, Bobby, and Bill found themselves outside, and they were still shaking from the events of the previous few minutes. They felt an odd mixture of elation and sadness. As Kovic later wrote,

> We had done it. It had been the biggest moment of our lives, we had shouted down the president of the United States and disrupted his acceptance speech. What more was there left to do but go home? I sat in my chair still shaking and began to cry.

Outside the 1972 Republican National Convention in Miami, the VVAW participates in a mass demonstration against President Nixon's handling of the Vietnam War.

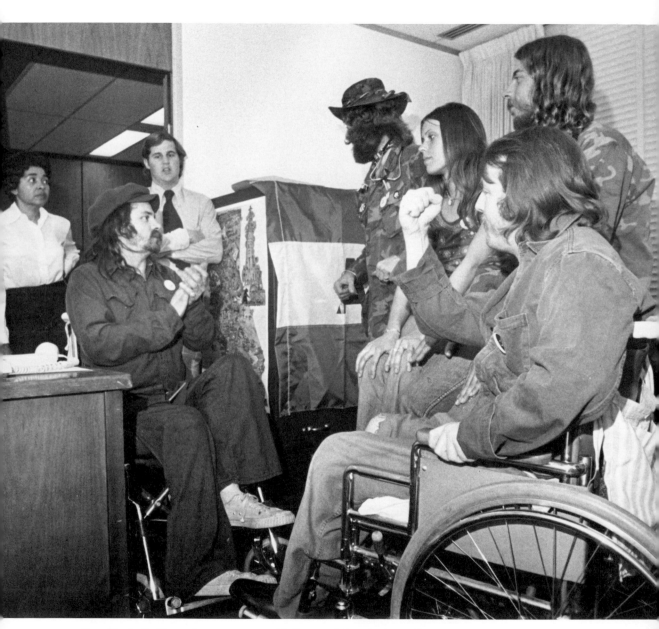

Ron Kovic (left) speaks to a group of fellow activists during a demonstration on February 12, 1974. The protesters occupied the office of California senator Alan Cranston to protest the conditions at the Long Beach Veterans Hospital.

8

NEW BATTLES

THE CONFUSING MIX OF EMOTIONS that Kovic felt as he left the Republican convention in Miami perhaps best characterizes his state of mind over the next decade and a half. It would be filled with incredible highs and terrible lows. He continued to demonstrate against the war, to speak out and make his unique voice heard, but still he felt the rage—rage over what he had suffered in Vietnam and rage over what he continued to suffer as a wounded veteran returned home.

As Kovic moved on with his life the nation moved on as well. In 1972, there was Ron Kovic leading a hunger strike in the offices of California senator Alan Cranston. Only a year later U.S. troops returned from Vietnam, and with the fall of Saigon in 1975, it seemed to be the perfect time for Ron to set his experiences down in writing. In simple English, he would try to tell his own story so that every American could understand what he and thousands of other veterans had gone through.

Ron Kovic sits with Dean Kahler, an activist who was wounded at Kent State in 1970. The two listen to plans to picket the Administration Building at the university on the seventh anniversary of the shootings.

That book became the highly acclaimed *Born on the Fourth of July.* He wrote the first manuscript in less than two months. Ironically, it was published in 1976, the year of the nation's bicentennial. Kovic's book provided just the right counterbalance to the nation's patriotic outpouring. Nineteen seventy-six was a year to celebrate America's great experiment in democracy, but it was no less a year to remember the occasions when that experiment had gone awry.

The book was an immediate success. *Newsweek* termed Kovic's "unabashed expression of feelings" a "form of bravery." C. B. D. Bryan, writing in the *New York Times,* referred to the book as "the most personal and honest testament published thus far by any young man who fought in the Vietnam War." Josiah Bunting recommended Ron's book to the readers of *Harper's* as a "personal chronicle of the national insanity."

In the summer of 1976, Kovic was asked to participate in the Democratic National Convention in New York City. Ron's appearance before the convention was a crowning achievement in a year that was already notable for the publication of his book. The two events together served to give him a heretofore unattained notoriety. When *Washington Post* reporter Philip McCombs traveled with Ron back to his hometown of Massapequa that August, Kovic expressed a feeling of contentment that had eluded him for many years. "It has been a long odyssey for me, a long journey through darkness" he told McCombs. Kovic continued,

> When I finished the book, I began to come out of eight years of incredible depression, nightmares, sickness, suicidal tendencies. I began to feel loving and existing for the first time since I came back from Vietnam.

Throughout the old neighborhood, friends approached Ron to say hello. Kovic was excited and elated by the reception the book was getting. "Did you see this ad in the *New York Times?*" he shouted to one neighbor. With a sense of real accomplishment setting in, Ron even indulged himself in a bit of overblown boasting. "The book is a work of art: a masterpiece," he told McCombs. "I think my book ranks up there with the greatest antiwar books ever written," he added, comparing *Born* with both *Johnny Got His Gun* and Erich Maria Remarque's *All Quiet on the Western Front* (1929).

After Grace, a woman who lived across the street from Ron's parents, called out her greetings, Ron informed his interviewer that until his book was published Grace had felt uncomfortable about speaking with him. Now she understood some of what he had gone through. Kovic was proud that his book was written in an accessible style that everyone could understand.

The American people, he was convinced, were seething about Vietnam. Though it did not show in their day-to-day lives, it was just under the surface, and if they would not talk about it, he would. After a decade of war, he stressed the need for a new focus on the spiritual needs of the nation. "I'm sure cancer could be cured, crippled men could walk again—if government priorities changed from adventure and profits and the military-industrial complex to people, health, spirituality. I could walk again if this society were truly a people society."

It was not long after the publication of *Born on the Fourth of July* before Hollywood came calling. Ron's agent phoned him one day to say that actor Al Pacino and producer Martin Bregman were interested in turning his book into a movie. A meeting was set up in Bregman's office, and Ron was quickly caught up in the roller-coaster ride of trying to pull together all the pieces of the production. Kovic described the experience to journalist Robert Sheer: "I remember their saying that they felt it could be a great film. Bregman hired a screenwriter. He came to the house once, in a limousine. My mom said the only time she saw a limousine was when people died."

Bregman brought in a young screenwriter named Oliver Stone to rewrite the script, and Kovic began working intensely with Pacino to help him prepare for the role. Kovic would party with Pacino at New York City's Studio 54 deep into the night, sleep until late the next morning, and then work all day. He described the "forty-five dollar hamburgers from room service" to Sheer: "It was the opposite of the rat-infested V.A. hospital. Hey, I was in Grace Slick's suite. I was somebody."

In the meantime, another picture roughly paralleling Kovic's experience moved into production. The film, *Coming Home* (1978), starred Jane Fonda, who had read Kovic's book and been moved by it, and Jon Voight. The movie dealt with a love affair between the wife of an enlisted man and a paraplegic veteran who has returned

from the war. Kovic was brought in as a consultant. Though the film was a critical success, even earning some Academy Awards, it did not do as well at the box office. Fearing that the movie version of *Born* would likewise not bring in great profits, Bregman's West German investors withdrew their support for the film. Four days before it was to go into production, the picture was put on hold.

Ron got different reasons for what had happened from various sources. Some claimed that Pacino had pulled out to pursue another film, *And Justice for All.* Others held that the arrival of new films dealing with the theme of Vietnam, such as *The Deer Hunter* and *Apocalypse Now,* had glutted the market and that audiences were tired of Vietnam. Whatever the reason, Kovic was crushed. As he told Jerry Parker of *Newsday,*

In this scene from the 1978 film Coming Home, *Jane Fonda (left) plays a hospital volunteer who falls in love with a disabled Vietnam veteran played by Jon Voight. Ron Kovic served as a consultant on the project.*

> I was numb. I felt the same way I felt when I lost a friend
> in Vietnam: shock, numb, didn't feel anything. I realized
> I could be destroyed in Hollywood as easily as I could be
> destroyed in Vietnam, and I left and went away and took
> a long trip.

Despondent over what had happened, Kovic flew to Atlanta, where he checked into a hotel that did not even have accommodations for his wheelchair. "I had to wash myself in the sink," Kovic told *Newsday.* It was, indeed, an odd choice of places to escape to, but he did not particularly care. He had never been to Atlanta before—that was reason enough to go. Kovic spent a week in his room, alone, trying to put the disappointment behind him.

Oliver Stone had told Kovic that if he ever made it big, "I'll come back for you." That day would come, but for now their relationship was tense. For a time, whenever they ran into each other in Los Angeles they would hurl accusations at one another about why the film had not been made. Kovic even threw a punch at Stone on one occasion.

What made matters worse was that, in Kovic's opinion, the other Vietnam pictures that had been released were not very good. He felt, along with many reviewers, that Michael Cimino's *The Deer Hunter* left "the taste of revenge in the mouth," and that its depiction of the Vietcong sent out a message of hate rather than a message of peace. He had seen *Apocalypse Now* at director Francis Ford Coppola's home in San Francisco but felt that the story was clumsy and, particularly at the end, marred by its ambiguity. What the American public needed, said Kovic in 1979, was another kind of picture. "*Born on the Fourth of July* is dangerous," he said, "because it deals with the victimization of one who is still alive and breathing. That is something people have a hard time with—that I'm still alive and they have to deal with me."

The next seven years were, by his own account, full of "wandering and drifting." In some ways that is an odd characterization of his life during this period. He maintained an active speaking schedule. He spoke on the radio regularly about military matters and war. One Memorial Day in Chicago, he went from getting arrested at an awards service, during which former Defense Secretary Robert McNamara was honored for "outstanding contributions to international understanding," to appearing beside Chicago mayor Jane Byrne as a special guest at another celebration. Kovic told a Chicago reporter that it was "the first time a political person such as myself went from the lock-up to the Ritz Carlton."

Ron even took on General William Westmoreland, who had commanded the U.S. troops in Vietnam, on the ABC morning show, "Good Morning America." But as in the first few years back from the war, it was during those quieter moments alone—alone with the knowledge of his injury that would never heal and the memory of the dead corporal from Georgia—that his depression resurfaced. It became a cycle: Ron would speak out in public to pull himself out of his private anguish. When he pulled back to carve out some space for himself once again, the despair would return.

Documentary filmmaker Loretta Smith has noted that this perhaps explains Kovic's penchant for missing his engagements. "I can't tell you how many times I've been

Director Francis Ford Coppola shakes hands with Ron Kovic on March 8, 1981, at a demonstration honoring Vietnam War veterans.

caught apologizing to groups that he promised he would show up for," Smith told *Newsday* writer Jon Kalish. "I end up getting called in the middle of the night by people who wondered what happened to Ron." Of Kovic's political work, Smith explained, "One problem with his activism is that it's always been so impulsive. It's been an emotional outlet as much as anything else."

One issue for which Kovic "got out there" was the Reagan administration's support for and military assistance to the government of El Salvador in the early 1980s. There, as in Vietnam a decade earlier, a civil war was in progress, and U.S. advisers were training the military and security police of the Salvadoran regime. That regime, headed by Roberto D'Aubuisson, flouted international human-rights laws and was renowned for its use of torture and other forms of repression to maintain its hold on power.

In 1983, Kovic helped to organize a three-day fast to protest U.S. policy in El Salvador. He was joined by clergy, politicians, and other veterans on a trip to the American Embassy in San Salvador, where the fast would take place. Before leaving, Kovic told *Newsweek*, "This is one of the most important missions in my life." He also wished to raise his voice against the use of U.S. military force in El Salvador because his younger brother Jack was now of military age, and Ron was determined that Jack would not end up in a wheelchair as he had.

All the while, Kovic continued to travel and keep odd hours. He told Ari Goldman of the *New York Times* in 1989, "Every time my monthly compensation check came in, I was on a jet." He would stay with friends or in cheap hotels, hopping from one location to another and never staying anywhere longer than six months. Throughout that time, Kovic continued to write. By 1983, he had set down some 2,200 pages of a major work he intended to publish as a trilogy entitled *After the War: An American Elegy*. The first book in the series would cover the war, the second his disillusionment, and the third the effect of the war on his hometown of Massapequa. To date it has not been published.

In 1984, Kovic published a novel titled *Around the World in Eight Days,* a surreal look at the trek of one veteran who bets that he can circle the globe without using an aircraft. In a review in the *Chicago Tribune,* Gerald Nicosia wrote that Kovic's book "bespeaks a great faith that life can be made better if we only try to do something noble and inspiring. It is this tempered-by-fire, courageous optimism that makes Kovic's voice so astonishingly original." Though other reviewers were equally impressed, the book did not achieve the popularity of *Born on the Fourth of July.*

By 1986, the combination of Kovic's emotional turmoil and his ceaseless wanderlust had taken its toll. He suffered a severe bladder infection, accompanied by a high fever, that forced him into the hospital for many months. By the time he got out, he was approaching his 40th birthday, and he decided that it was about time "to stop running and put down roots." He bought a three-bedroom ranch house in Los Angeles and took up gardening. He found a renewed sense of energy. "I bought a piano," he told the *New York Times*'s Ari Goldman, "and began to play. I started painting in acrylics on 40-foot canvases 5 feet high."

He was genuinely happy for perhaps the first time since his triumphant address before the Democratic National Convention. "I lived very privately, alone, by myself," he said. "I had friends, but they respected my privacy."

A year later one of those friends had the audacity to intrude on that privacy. It was Oliver Stone. Fresh from his success with his films *Platoon* and *Wall Street,* Stone had three words for Kovic: "Ronnie, I'm ready."

Ron Kovic arrives with his father at the 1990 Academy Awards ceremony. Kovic's screenplay for Born on the Fourth of July, *cowritten with Oliver Stone, was nominated for an Oscar.*

9

BORN ON THE FOURTH OF JULY

FINALLY, RON'S STORY would make it to the screen. His previous experience had been so disappointing that he almost did not dare to believe that it would actually happen this time. The critical and commercial success of *Platoon,* however, showed that Americans still felt deeply about the war in Vietnam, and Oliver Stone, who had directed that film, had longstanding ties to the Kovic work.

Stone called Kovic about the project in the summer of 1986. For the next three years, Kovic would be intimately involved in all aspects of the film, from cowriting the screenplay with Stone to casting the crucial role of his own character in the picture. In the latter regard, both men were lucky to find a willing participant in the young Hollywood star Tom Cruise.

Cruise was drawn to Kovic's story, he said, because of its relevance to his own life. "I felt like Ron Kovic could have been me," he told Robert Sheer. Cruise was a young boy living in Canada during the

Vietnam War, and when he came on board to do the film version of *Born* he still had only a rough understanding of the war. He recalled moving back to the United States in the mid-1970s and trying to piece together what had happened. He remembered seeing some young children who were arguing over the meaning of the war. They appeared to be divided. One held that the United States had been terribly defeated, another asserted that the Americans had won the war, and still another boy wondered aloud, "What is Vietnam?"

If working on the film presented an opportunity to educate himself in greater depth about this pivotal event in U.S. history, Cruise first had to overcome Kovic's misgivings about his suitability for the role. "I had my doubts," Kovic remembers. But they were quickly dispelled after he met Cruise, in whom he detected great "insight" about what he had gone through. He had never fully felt that with Pacino. For his own part, Stone felt good about the casting from the beginning. "I saw similarities between Ron and Tom. They were both working-class Catholics with somewhat similar backgrounds. They were both obsessed with excellence—perhaps too much so."

Looking at Cruise was a disturbing experience for Kovic the first time he came to visit the set. The production designers had constructed an alarmingly accurate version of Kovic's parents' home. As Ron entered and looked at Cruise from behind, he did not recognize the younger actor sitting in the wheelchair. Kovic, then 43 years old, was taken aback as the man turned around: "With his long hair and moustache, he looked just like me."

Great effort was taken to fully prepare Cruise for the role prior to shooting the film. Kovic and Cruise worked closely with each other from the beginning of 1987 through the end of shooting in August 1989. Cruise, who spent day after day in a wheelchair to better understand the reality of Kovic's paralysis, found the work exhausting.

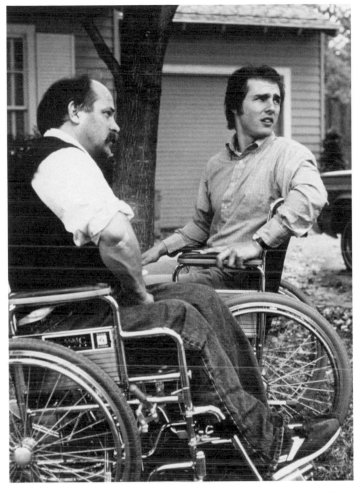

Ron Kovic helps Tom Cruise prepare for the filming of Born on the Fourth of July. *Cruise won Kovic's respect by spending many hours in a wheelchair to gain insight into the role.*

His admiration for Kovic grew as he spent more time with him. "The kind of courage that these people have makes you realize what the human soul is capable of in terms of surviving," Cruise told Sheer.

Once, when the two men were visiting a veterans' hospital in southern California, Cruise was unsure whether it would be appropriate to sit in the chair. They were in the workout room, and Cruise told Kovic, "I don't want to offend anybody."

Kovic responded, "You won't offend anyone. I think they'll respect you because you're going to learn about

how difficult their lives are." Repeatedly, Cruise would
come face to face with the difficulties and prejudices
encountered daily by disabled Americans. Cruise recalls
one incident in particular:

> I remember I was going around with Kovic and I was in
> the wheelchair. I went into this high-tech gift shop, and
> this girl comes up to me and says, "Excuse me, sir, I am
> very sorry, but could you please stop rolling around on our
> carpet, or I'm going to have to ask you to leave." I said,
> "Why?" She said, "Your tires are leaving marks." I could
> not believe it.

As Cruise's admiration for Kovic grew during his preparation for the film, Kovic came to find in Cruise a real
friend. Later during production, as they prepared to shoot
a scene in which Ron, just returned from the VA hospital,
lashes out in despair at his mother, Cruise asked Kovic to
act out the scene first. Stone cleared the set of everyone
except for himself, Cruise, and Ron. As he read the lines—
his own words—Kovic began to feel very uncomfortable.
As Kovic tells the story, "I'm not an actor but I'm very
emotional, and I became very, very loud and very impas-
sioned. I gave every single thing I had, as if it was happening again." The trauma of reliving that painful experience
was more than he could take. He fled from the house in
which they were shooting as soon as they had finished.

He got into a car the film company had provided for him
and asked the driver to go—anywhere, he just wanted to
get out of there. Soon he noticed a Jeep pull up alongside
of his car. He looked over to see that it was Cruise, who
rolled down his window and yelled at Ron, "What are you
doing to me, Kovic?" Ron responded, "You're making me
depressed." Cruise shot back, "You're making *me* depressed." Says Kovic, "It was a crazy scene. We were
laughing and cursing and shouting and screaming." Kovic
told journalist Robert Seidenberg,

> I wondered if I had it inside me to get through this, and
> then, all of a sudden, I realized I wasn't alone. Tom Cruise

was agonizing over this part, and he didn't know if he could go on, either. All of a sudden, I realized that Cruise understood.

Because it was too expensive to shoot the film on Long Island, an exact replica of Kovic's street was re-created in Texas, where much of the movie was shot. Kovic remembers his delight at meeting the cast members for the film, who would be playing the many people he had written about in his book, including the kids who were playing his friends from childhood. Kovic told *American Film,* "Some of them, including Bryan Larkin, who played little Ronnie Kovic, had come from Massapequa, my hometown on Long Island. They were so sweet, so beautiful."

If meeting with the kids was the fun part of Kovic's movie experience, watching the filming of the home-coming parade was simply wrenching. He had expected it to be relatively painless, but as the marchers and the procession reappeared out of his memory onto the road in front of him, Ron found himself deeply affected. Suddenly, he had a vivid sense of the depth of his own loss, not now, but as a 21-year-old marine returned from war.

> I can see now how brave I had tried to be—*tried* to be—and what a front I had put on for my parents, trying to sit tall in the car when we came home. I saw what a sad day it had been. And I also saw how courageous my parents had been.

When Ron's parents came to visit him in Dallas toward the end of the filming, it was an important moment for him. He felt that until that year, in the course of making the movie, he had not understood how they, too, had suffered. Focused so intently on his own experience, he had shielded himself from his parents' pain over his injuries in Vietnam. "I guess I just blocked it out for years. I didn't want to feel what they must have gone through." Kovic continued,

> I began to realize that, my God, the young men are not the only victims of war. War reaches all the way back into the community, it wounds the most unlikely. And it's the

mothers and fathers and the people who lived across the street from us, everybody that I had ever touched as a young man in that town was hurt and wounded when I was hurt and wounded.

Kovic acknowledged to *American Film* in 1990 that because of his own bitterness, his parents could not reach out to him when he had most needed it. It had taken years before he could honestly discuss with them his true feelings. Thus, the film provided Ron an opportunity for reconciliation with his parents and the rest of his family. They came to visit on the day the crew was filming inside the Dallas Convention Center, where the scenes depicting Ron's confrontation with President Nixon at the 1972 Republican convention were being shot. Kovic enthusiastically recounts how his parents jumped into the middle of the action and were included in the film as extras.

Tom Cruise, Ron Kovic, and Oliver Stone celebrate backstage after Born on the Fourth of July *sweeps most of the top prizes at the 1990 Golden Globe Awards.*

By the time the film was finished, says Cruise, it had become a cause. As he told Robert Sheer,

> I'm proud of the movie. I don't want people thinking this is just another Vietnam movie. It's a film that tells us we can't blindly trust the leaders of this country, that we ourselves must search and find out where we stand and what we believe in. It's not easy finding the truth about anything. Whether people are left or right, we've tried to make an honest movie.

Born on the Fourth of July opened around the country in December 1989 to mixed reviews. Vincent Canby, in the *New York Times,* heralded the film as a work "of enormous visceral power." As if in response to Kovic's own criticism of the earlier Vietnam films, Canby added, "It's the most ambitious nondocumentary film yet made about the entire Vietnam experience. More effectively than Hal Ashby's 'Coming Home' and even Michael Cimino's 'The Deer Hunter,' it connects the war of arms with the war of conscience at home."

Commercially, the film scored very well, and Stone received an Academy Award for Best Director, though the film lost out to *Driving Miss Daisy* for Best Picture. Nor did Ron's screenplay with Stone, nominated for an Oscar, get the nod. Although just being nominated for an Oscar would have been quite an achievement for Kovic, he and Stone won a Golden Globe Award for Best Screenplay, and the film took three more Golden Globes for best drama, best director, and best actor.

For Ron Kovic, the reviews and accolades were not the measure by which the film would be judged. His mind was on the thousands, perhaps millions, of young students who might benefit from his experience. As he told Robert Seidenberg,

> Working on the script with Oliver was the first time that I began to understand that my sacrifice, my paralysis, the difficulties, the frustrations, the impossibilities of each and every day would now be for something very valuable,

In October 1990, Ron Kovic speaks out to protest the U.S. military buildup in preparation for war in the Persian Gulf. Two decades after his own disabling injury, Ron Kovic continues to be a powerful voice for peace.

something that would help protect the young people of this country from having to go through what I went through.

Soon after *Born on the Fourth of July* had been completed, Kovic joined 200 students at Loyola Marymount University in Los Angeles for a screening of the film. He entered the auditorium quietly during the middle of the film, without the knowledge of the students. When it ended, Kovic found himself sobbing uncontrollably. When the students realized that he was in the room with them, they proceeded to give him a five-minute standing ovation.

Completely overcome with emotion, Ron cried harder than he had in years as the cheering continued, and he stayed for an hour to answer questions. It was undeniably the climax of a fantastic journey he had undertaken to share his pain with others, and through that sharing to find peace of mind from the horrors he had seen, from the atrocities he had been forced to commit, and from the suffering he had experienced. No longer blinded by hurt, he was finally in a position to see the positive effect his life could have on others. Kovic told *Newsday,*

> For a long time I was very angry. I was very bitter. The anger and the bitterness has left me. I feel very thankful to be alive, to be Ron Kovic. I never thought I would say this, but I believe that my wound has become a blessing in disguise. It's enabled me to reach millions of people with a message of peace and a message of hope.

Kovic moved on from the experience of *Born on the Fourth of July* to set his sights on new challenges. He was commissioned by the Vietnam Veterans Ensemble Theater Company (VETCO) to create a play based on his as-yet unpublished novel, *An American Elegy,* with John Di Fusco, another vet and the author of the acclaimed play *Tracers.* But no matter what endeavor he would move on to, Ron had redefined the meaning of heroism for future generations.

Whereas in past decades young boys and girls sat in the movies watching John Wayne and Audie Murphy make armed conflict look exciting and heroic, they now could see the true story of Ron Kovic and learn that war is no game. That accomplishment put all the years since Kovic's injury into perspective. As Kovic himself put it in a recent interview,

> It has been a tremendously difficult and painful life, but I have never felt happier. I have never felt stronger. There has never been more love in my heart. I have never had more hope for humanity and more hope for my own life than I do now. I wouldn't trade places with any other person at any other time.

FURTHER READING

Baker, Mark. *Nam.* New York: Morrow, 1981.

Chomsky, Noam, and Edward S. Herman. *Manufacturing Consent.* New York: Pantheon Books, 1988.

————. *The Washington Connection and Third World Fascism.* Boston: South End Press, 1979.

Crane, Stephen. *The Red Badge of Courage.* New York: Bantam, 1981.

Fitzgerald, Frances. *Fire in the Lake.* Boston: Little, Brown, 1972.

Gitlin, Todd. *The Sixties: Years of Hope, Days of Rage.* New York: Bantam Books, 1987.

Halberstam, David. *The Making of a Quagmire: America & Vietnam During the Kennedy Era.* New York: Knopf, 1987.

Herr, Michael. *Dispatches.* New York: Knopf, 1968.

Hodgson, Godfrey. *America in Our Time.* New York: Random House, 1976.

Karnow, Stanley. *Vietnam: A History.* New York: Penguin Books, 1983.

Kovic, Ron. *Born on the Fourth of July.* New York: McGraw-Hill, 1976.

Patterson, James. *America in the Twentieth Century.* New York: Harcourt Brace Jovanovich, 1983.

Remarque, Erich Maria. *All Quiet on the Western Front.* Hauppauge, NY: Barron's, 1984.

Schell, Jonathan. *The Time of Illusion.* New York: Knopf, 1976.

Trumbo, Dalton. *Johnny Got His Gun.* New York: Bantam, 1984.

Weinstein, James. *The Decline of Socialism in America.* New York: Monthly Review Press, 1967.

CHRONOLOGY

1946   Born Ron Kovic on July 4 in Ladysmith, Wisconsin

1951   Moves with family to Massapequa, Long Island

1964   Enlists in the U.S. Marines

1965–66   Completes first tour of duty in Vietnam

1968   Spine severed during heavy shelling in second tour; recuperates in veterans' hospital in Bronx, New York; returns home to Massapequa and participates in parade in his honor on July 4

1969   Goes to Mexican village of Las Fuentas; returns home and spends six months in a VA hospital after breaking leg

1970   Joins antiwar movement following killings at Kent State University

1971   Moves to Los Angeles, California, in January and becomes active in Vietnam Veterans Against the War

1972   Shouts down President Nixon at the Republican National Convention in Miami

1972–76   Leads protests to call attention to conditions in VA hospitals

1976   Publishes *Born on the Fourth of July* and addresses the Democratic National Convention in New York City

1978   After beginning work on a film version of *Born on the Fourth of July* with Al Pacino, the production is suddenly put on hold; consults on the film *Coming Home*

1979–85   Works on mammoth war novel, *After the War: An American Elegy*; the 2,200-page work is not published

1980–83   Participates in a variety of activist work against the draft and for peace in Central America

1984   Publishes the novel *Around the World in Eight Days*

1987   Director Oliver Stone begins production of a film version of *Born on the Fourth of July*, starring Tom Cruise as Ron Kovic; Kovic helps Cruise prepare for the role

1989   The film *Born on the Fourth of July* is released

1990   Kovic wins Golden Globe Award for screenplay cowritten with Stone

INDEX

INDEX

PICTURE CREDITS

Nathaniel Moss graduated from Brown University with a B.A. in American Civilization. After completing a journalism internship with *The Nation* magazine, he served as a speech writer for the late U.S. Representative Ted Weiss of New York. He is currently a freelance writer living in New York City.

Jerry Lewis is the National Chairman of the Muscular Dystrophy Association (MDA) and host of the MDA Labor Day Telethon. An internationally acclaimed comedian, Lewis began his entertainment career in New York and then performed in a comedy team with singer and actor Dean Martin from 1946 to 1956. Lewis has appeared in many films—including *The Delicate Delinquent, Rock a Bye Baby, The Bellboy, Cinderfella, The Nutty Professor, The Disorderly Orderly,* and *The King of Comedy*—and his comedy performances continue to delight audiences around the world.

John Callahan is a nationally syndicated cartoonist and the author of an illustrated autobiography, *Don't Worry, He Won't Get Far on Foot.* He has also produced three cartoon collections: *Do Not Disturb Any Further, Digesting the Child Within,* and *Do What He Says! He's Crazy!!!* He has recently been the subject of feature articles in the *New York Times Magazine,* the *Los Angeles Times Magazine,* and the Cleveland *Plain Dealer* and has been profiled on "60 Minutes." Callahan resides in Portland, Oregon.